10-Minute Power Tips for Parents

Raising Secure Kids in an Anxious World

"Sheri's book is simple and profound, with information laid out in an everyday, easy-to-read format. She gives practical daily advice packed with lots of additional resources as well as examples of how to incorporate the advice into daily life."

—*Topaz Cadena, mother of three boys*

"In *10-Minute Power Tips for Parents,* Sheri provides many gems on parenting that will enrich your relationships with your children and unify your family! She gives such practical advice you can integrate into your life to help you be more intentional about being the best parent you can be for your children. Her words will inspire you and challenge you as a parent to live a life that leads your children to walk closely with God and continually grow in Him."

—*Beth Law, mother of two*

"I am so excited about this book! It is a really insightful refresher on parenting, life, and the ways to keep all areas in balance. We need to slow life down and make sure that first things really are first. There are topics in it not everyone talks about enough, and enlightening perspective on what really matters. Sheri Schaefer is full of wisdom. She's real, and I think everyone must read this book!"

—*Joanna Swaggart, mother of three*

"I really liked this book. I especially liked the chapters 'Let Your

Kids Fail' and 'Learn to Say I'm Sorry.' There are very good examples in this book that help you understand the concepts being presented in a practical way."

—*Dennell Maestas, mother of six, grandmother of one*

"I really like how Sheri makes it applicable in the 'Take a Step' section of each chapter and guides you through the prayer so you are praying specific prayers! I love how in the 'Are You Having Fun?' chapter it reminds me that even though there are hard times we experience, we can still rejoice and choose to have fun and not be shaken. This teaches our children that we can trust God!"

—*Melissa Hordes, mother of three*

10-Minute

POWER TIPS

Raising Secure Kids in an Anxious World

A 31-DAY DEVOTIONAL FOR PARENTS

Sheri Schaefer

with **MEG SCHAEFER**

Editing and Proofreading: Sally Hanan and Liz Smith of Inksnatcher.com
Cover Design and Interior Layout: Allison Metcalfe

Ordering Information: Quantity sales. Special discounts are available on quantity purchases by corporations, associations, and others. For details, contact the author at the email address previously listed.

10-Minute Power Tips: Raising Secure Kids in an Anxious World/Sheri Schaefer
ISBN 978-1-7333330-0-9
eBook ISBN 978-1-7333330-1-6

Table of Contents

*For best results read just one day at a time so you have time to think about what you read and then how to best implement it. However, feel free to jump around if one day's topic is exactly what you are facing.

Dedication

This book is dedicated to Colleen Cawthon. When my children were in grade school and Colleen didn't have children yet, she asked me on several occasions, "When are you going to write a book on parenting?" At the time, I had absolutely no earthly idea why she would be asking me that because I felt like I was doing good just to keep my head above water. But all those years ago, she planted a seed, a thought in my mind, and now over thirty years since those words were spoken, I have written a book on parenting, and I have been able to share the wisdom I have received along the way. Colleen is in heaven now rejoicing with her King and probably saying, "What took you so long?" Colleen, I still see your smile and hear your laughter and see you in your beautiful children.

I also want to dedicate this book to my incredible parents who had such wisdom in knowing how to direct me with my personality in the way I should go. They were such a good example of love, discipline, fun, and adventure.

And, of course, this is also dedicated to the one I love and have been committed to since 1972: my husband, Mike Schaefer, who has been such a good balance for me and a good example of passion and strength to our children.

I dedicate this book to you, the reader, also. I am believing that you will be blessed and strengthened as you read this devotional. Knowing how busy you parents in the thick of it are, I wanted to do the study and research for you and give you a fuller and deeper knowledge on these subjects.

Introduction

The purpose of this book is to be an encouragement to parents. I think parenting is the most important job we will ever have while we are on earth. For me, it was the hardest job I have had—and I've had several jobs. The reason parenting is so difficult, I believe, is that it is a 24-7, pretty much nonstop job, with the exception of some date nights, Mother's Day outings, or a weekend getaway with a spouse. However, it is also difficult because to raise a well-mannered, disciplined child, *you,* the parent, need to be disciplined and selfless yourself.

The age difference between my brother and me is seven years. Not long after he was born, I started school, and when I was in middle school, he was just starting school. Needless to say, I didn't learn a lot about sharing and not getting my own way because of the big difference in age. My first years of marriage were no picnic for me nor my husband in so many ways, but it was really through parenting that the Lord began to help me see the lack of discipline and selfishness in my own life. It has been a lifelong challenge to overcome.

I hope the stories and the lessons learned, interlaced with a little humor, and the wisdom I have gleaned from the Bible will help you avoid some of the pitfalls I encountered and realize the importance of parenting well. I have also included resources that will help you go deeper into and study further the subjects you need more insight and wisdom on.

Thoughts from My Kids

PHOTO BY WORRELL PHOTOGRAPHY

I am truly thankful for who my parents are and what they taught me growing up! Now that I am a husband and father of two little girls, I often think back to my childhood and desire to instill the same principles in my girls. I think of the fun memories, lessons learned, and good habits that still live on today. I know we pass on more to our children by how we live than by the words we teach. This truth really causes me to step back from time to time and evaluate if the life I am living today in front of my girls is a life built on the habits and convictions I want guiding them.

I am thankful for my mother creating healthy habits in me and for her joy in life—habits like no sugary cereals or candy in the pantry or that "more water" was the answer to almost any ailment. As I have grown up, from college to starting a family, I have often heard her voice in my head when feeling overwhelmed: "You need to stop thinking about this on today's emotions and go get some rest." Wow, who would have known that a little sleep could solve a life spiraling out of control?

My father inspired one of the greatest gifts I have in life—a personal and very real relationship with Jesus. His relationship influenced everything, from reading daily devotions to taking someone in off the street for a night. There was no limit to showing God's love or obeying His prompting. My father's love for God surpassed any religious duties or requirements. I still remember waking up some mornings in our second-story home to the feeling of a gentle shaking because Dad was in his room upstairs dancing, or on his knees praying, or singing his love and devotion before his Savior. I knew my dad had lived some wild days, and I could save many years of learning from his findings.

My parents spoke wisdom and favor over my life so often I believed it. I hope this parenting devotional can be a similar inspiration to creating habits in your family!

—Shaun Schaefer

PHOTO BY MEGAN KAMAUOHA

I think you'll find this book inspiring and full of practical information. My mom has been told many times she should write a book on family and parenting. What an honor it is to be able to raise kids in a healthy, happy environment and help instill in them things that will help shape their lives now and throughout their lifetimes. I believe this quick, easy-to-read, follow-and-apply book and format will not only help you get good information but also use it.

Some of my favorite memories growing up are of my mom reading to us on road trips, special vacations together (then and now), and the many habits both parents helped me form at an early age (like daily time with God and reading His Word; setting goals: physically, spiritually, mentally, and financially; learning to trust God and believe for big things; and keeping your word, even to your own hurt). My dad would let us ride on his back and play hide-and-go-seek with us. (He still does with my kids.) We'd have family nights where we'd do crafts or play games and have special times of worship and prayer as a family. So many special lessons, principles, and memories I have and am still making with my parents!

Having my own family now, I know how intentional you have to be to make and have those special times, but I know how special and important they are. I hope you enjoy and apply many of these ideas and principles into your family ways and how you parent. May they give you creative ideas and bless and help you in your journey.

—Sarah Schaefer Kimberly

Perfection Not Required

*I am not trying to please people. I want to please God.
Do you think I am trying to please people? If I were
doing that, I would not be a servant of Christ.*

GALATIANS 1:10 CEV

We all want to be perfect parents. We want to produce perfect kids in
a perfect home in a perfect life. With our access to social media, we are
bombarded daily with a false image of perfection portrayed by other
people's highlight reel—not their real, everyday lives. Our exposure
to social media, the internet, TV, and the like builds an unrealistic
standard for us to compare ourselves with. It's not healthy, and it's not
real!

I didn't deal with social media smokescreens when my kids were
little, but I did impose a perfection expectation on myself. The more
I started seeing myself aiming for perfection on a regular basis, the
more I became frustrated. In God's Word I began to see that what was
pleasing to Him was not perfection but doing things with excellence
and as unto Him. "Whatever you do, do it from the heart for the Lord
and not for the people" (Colossians 3:23 CEB).

One thing that usually accompanies our desire to be perfect is that
we begin to compare ourselves with other people. When we compare
who we are or what we have with other people, the Bible says we're

not being wise: "For we dare not class ourselves or compare ourselves with those who commend themselves. But they, measuring themselves by themselves, and comparing themselves among themselves, are not wise" (2 Corinthians 10:12 NKJV).

Lucifer was the first perfectionist. " Thou wast perfect in thy ways from the day that thou wast created, till iniquity was found in thee" (Ezekiel 28:15 KJV).

In Steve Foss's book *Satan's Dirty Little Secret*, he says, "In this state of absolute perfection a most horrific event took place. Lucifer got his eyes off of God and onto himself. He began to compare himself with God and with others. He saw that God's beauty surpassed his own. With creation, he realized his beauty and brightness was unmatched. He felt inferior to God and superior to others."[1]

How you are fallen from heaven,
O Lucifer, son of the morning!
How you are cut down to the ground,
You who weakened the nations!
For you have said in your heart:
"I will ascend into heaven,
I will exalt my throne above the stars of God;
I will also sit on the mount of the congregation
On the farthest sides of the north;
I will ascend above the heights of the clouds,
I will be like the Most High."
ISAIAH 14:12-14 NKJV

We can learn from this situation that when pride, comparison, and a desire to be perfect start to become the norm, it can be quite

---

1   Steve Foss, *Satan's Dirty Little Secret* (Lake Mary, FL: Charisma House, 2012), 19.

disastrous. I believe social media is a perfect place for all this to incubate—if we let it. When we realize that being a good parent is not being a perfect parent but one who depends on God for His wisdom and grace, stays thankful, and keeps God in first place in our lives, we can rest in the knowledge that that is what makes us successful in His eyes.

My main point in this chapter is to help you realize that though you may have never been a parent before, and your child has never been a child before, none of us are perfect, and that's okay. We are learning how to be excellent in what we are doing. God doesn't require us to be perfect.

Only one perfect person lived on earth, and that was Jesus Christ. So many times we impose unrealistic expectations upon ourselves as to how our house should look, how we should look, or how our kids should look and act. As we get our eyes back on the Lord and show forth His grace and character in our lives, we truly will live a freer and more satisfying life.

If I can leave you with one word as I end this chapter, it would be the word *laugh*. Learn to laugh at yourself and your kids at times instead of taking everything so seriously. It is only by and through God's grace that we are able to be God's representative to our children and to do that well.

Take a Step

Are you a perfectionist? Are there areas of your life that cause you distress because they aren't perfect? Are you frustrated about this because of your own desire for perfection or because of wanting to appear perfect to others? There is a difference between striving for excellence and striving for perfection. Do you know the difference?

Take some time to filter through the areas of your life you've put under your own magnifying glass, causing frustration. Are you hoping for things to be perfect or excellent?

Lean In

Father, I have very high hopes and expectations to live an excellent life. I desire the kind of life you have planned for me. But I also know that perfection is not reality. Help me to operate in excellence by being infused with your supernatural power, favor, and ability. I know I need you, and I thank you for being with me and helping me. In Jesus's name, amen.

Digging Deeper

· *Satan's Dirty Little Secret* by Steve Foss

"24/7: Once you sign on to be a mother that's the only shift they offer."

Notes

Learn to Say, "I'm Sorry"

> For You, Lord, are good, and ready to forgive, and abundant in mercy to all those who call upon You.
>
> **PSALM 86:5 NKJV**

Let's face it, there are times when we blow it as parents, plain and simple. Usually it is because we get tired and impatient with the kids or we're in a stressful situation. One very important thing for us to remember about parenting is we are constantly modeling behavior right before our children's eyes. We are modeling the good, the bad, and the ugly!

When my kids were little, the Lord impressed upon me that when I yelled at or became impatient with the children, I needed to be quick to say I was sorry. Most days parenting is so routine, so monotonous, so *unending*. Our days seem never ending because of how many times we repeat ourselves over and over in the same day. Training our children involves a lot of repetition, which is the way they learn—by doing things over and over again. This can be a slow process, to say the least—especially if you are in a hurry to go someplace and they aren't.

When Mike or I told the children we were sorry for getting impatient, raising our voices, or not keeping our word, it was not only the right thing to do but it taught them that apologizing for something helps keep pride from entering into their lives. It keeps their relationship with God and with others healthy. It also softens the hurt their words may have caused.

Humility is something gained and practiced as we grow in wisdom and grace. *Easton's 1897 Bible Dictionary* defines *humility* as "a prominent Christian grace. . . . It is a state of mind well pleasing to God; it preserves the soul in tranquility, . . . and makes us patient under trials."[1]

> Likewise, you who are younger, be subject to the elders. Clothe yourselves, all of you, with humility toward one another for "God opposes the proud but gives grace to the humble."
> **1 PETER 5:5 ESV**

> He leads the humble in what is right, and teaches the humble his way.
> **PSALM 25:9 ESV**

As parents, when we humble ourselves to say we are sorry when we're wrong or when we have inappropriate behavior toward anyone, we are teaching our children to do the same thing. We are also showing them that in any relationship we are involved in, we need to extend God's forgiveness and grace to people as we receive His grace and forgiveness in our own lives.

Our children are watching how we treat and value others all the time, whether it is the clerk at the grocery store or an angry driver. Life is all about being quick to forgive and to extend His grace and mercy to ourselves and to others.

Love and humility go hand in hand. It is by spending time with God

---

1   *Easton's Bible Dictionary*, s.v. "Humility," accessed June 7, 2019, https://www.biblegateway.com/resources/eastons-bible-dictionary/Humility.

in prayer and reflection each day that we have the power and strength to walk in love and humility when dealing with our children.

> We ought not to be weary of doing little things for the love of God, who regards not the greatness of the work but the love with which it is performed.
> **BROTHER LAWRENCE**

Take a Step

Be quick to apologize. Saying sorry to your kids and taking responsibility for your actions does not empower them or give them control in your relationship. Humility produces great fruit and promotes us. When we humble ourselves, it puts us in a position to be honored. And as we quickly take responsibility for our wrongful or hurtful words, it trains us to be better and more cautious with our reactions. Likewise, it becomes a habit or way of doing things for our kids. They observe and learn it is normal and expected to identify when they have said something wrong and to take responsibility for their actions.

Lean In

Father, there is no greater gift than your love and acceptance. I know the immediate result of that love is forgiveness. Thank you for sending your precious Son to pay the price for my wrongs. Thank you, Jesus, for shedding your pure, perfect blood for me. I will live to honor that sacrifice by being quick to forgive and to ask for forgiveness. I humble myself at your feet, Father, to ask for help. I position myself to receive mercy and help from you to extend mercy to others. In Jesus's name, amen.

· *Practicing the Presence of God* by Brother Lawrence

> *"When I raise my voice, my kids call it yelling, but I call it motivational speaking for the select of hearing."*

Notes

DAY THREE

Work Ethic

The Lord will open to you his good treasury, the heavens, to give the rain to your land in its season and to bless all the work of your hands. And you shall lend to many nations, but you shall not borrow.

DEUTERONOMY 28:12 ESV

Most people will go through life needing a job or a career. This being the case, it seems logical that a critical part of training children is equipping them to be excellent workers. It is glaringly obvious when someone has not been taught a good work ethic.

This training can start with preschool-age children. As soon as they begin to play with toys, they can learn how to put them away. I know several parents who have a rule that their kids must put away one toy or group of toys (e.g., blocks, Legos, or a puzzle) before getting out another. Preschool children can also help put plates on or off the table to set or clear it, throw the trash away, bring diapers to their mom, help clean their room, and put clothes in the hamper to be washed.

From the elementary-age child and up, you can increase the amount and level of household duties they do. This is all about training and preparing them to one day be on their own—living successfully and fully equipped to be part of the workforce, working in whatever area God calls and gifts them to.

Mike and I felt our kids needed to do some chores because they were part of a family and that is what families do—work together. As they got older, we wanted to teach them about money management. We decided to pay them, beginning in elementary school, so they would learn how to manage their money. You can incorporate this in several different ways into your children's lives. For example, get three containers or piggy banks and mark one as "Save 10%," one as "Give 10%," and the third as "Spend." When you pay your children, they can put the designated amounts into the first two containers, and the rest goes into their spending-money container. When you do this from a very early age, you begin to teach them how to be good stewards of what God has blessed them with.

GIVE 10%
SAVE 10%

When acted upon, these principles will help set the course for the rest of their lives. One of the three primary reasons couples get divorced or have marriage problems is because of financial difficulties and overwhelming debt. When we start at an early age to teach our children to give 10 percent and save 10 percent, and they manage the rest wisely, we are setting them up for success in several areas of life.

When Sarah was in middle school, we helped enroll her in a Red Cross class for babysitting that included CPR. She was able to babysit quite a bit while she was in middle school and some in high school, until she got very involved in playing volleyball. At that time Shaun took over a few of her jobs—until he realized he liked mowing lawns and doing odd jobs better than babysitting. Having these jobs helped them put gas in their cars and have some pocket change in addition to their allowances. When they were in high school, we gave them a set amount of money for them to manage their expenses. This really helped them to learn to manage their money before they were away at college.

One book I found to be one of the best for helping parents

know the age-appropriate practical living skills kids can perform is *What Every Child Should Know Along the Way* by Gail Martin. It is excellent for knowing which life skills to teach in every stage of life as well as how to teach children about personal safety, manners, gifts and talents, biblical character traits, cultivating family unity, and dynamic devotional living. It is well worth adding to your investment in continuing-education materials for parenting.

One essential thing to remember is that we as parents are to be lifelong learners. I would read articles from Christian magazines and books and would talk with older women about what I was facing throughout the many different seasons of parenting; however, I always come back to the Bible to make sure what I was doing lined up with His Word. He being God the Father, who created us all, certainly knows how we all can function best, and He left instructions for that in His Word. Our job is to find out those principles and be doers of them.

Numerous Scriptures talk about work and the rewards of work:

✔ "The wise man saves for the future, but the foolish man spends whatever he gets" (Proverbs 21:20 TLB).

✔ "A slack hand causes poverty, but the hand of the diligent makes rich" (Proverbs 10:4 ESV).

✔ "The Lord God took the man and put him in the garden of Eden to work and keep it" (Genesis 2:15 ESV).

✔ "Slothfulness casts into a deep sleep, and an idle person will suffer hunger" (Proverbs 19:15 ESV).

✔ "Whoever works his land will have plenty of bread, but he who follows worthless pursuits lacks sense" (Proverbs 12:11 ESV).

✔ "[God] is a rewarder of those who diligently seek Him" (Hebrews 11:6 NKJV).

✔ "Whatever you do, work at it with all your heart, as working for the Lord, not for human masters, since you know that you will receive an inheritance from the Lord as a reward. It is the Lord Christ you are serving" (Colossians 3:23 NIV).

These are good Scriptures, and there are many more to study with your children about work and the rewards of work.

Take a Step

Set up a family economy inside your home. Designate age-appropriate chores, and then set up a reward system. Explain to your kids the biblical reasons for tithing and giving and why we need to save money. Tell them when you're going to tithe and talk about something you are saving money for. It is not appropriate to discuss family finances with younger children, but you can give them an idea of when and how you are making smart financial decisions.

Lean In

Father, we are so blessed and we are so thankful to you. You have abundantly blessed us with our children, our home, and so much more. We want to be good stewards of that blessing. We choose to tithe as a representation of our covenant with you. We know you promise to bless all we put our hand to. We are thankful for our jobs and bless our bosses. Thank you for an atmosphere of thanksgiving in our home. We love to work, and we love to play. Help us create that atmosphere and balance in our home. In Jesus's name, amen.

Digging Deeper

- *The ABCs of Handling Money God's Way* by Howard and Bev Dayton: Crown Ministries
- *What Every Child Should Know Along the Way* by Gail Martin

"It is amazing how quickly the kids learn to drive a car yet are unable to understand the lawnmower, snow blower, or vacuum cleaner."

Notes

More Notes

First Things First

> *Seek first the kingdom of God and His righteousness,*
> *and all these things shall be added to you.*
>
> **MATTHEW 6:33 NKJV**

Parenting is one of the hardest things I have done. I don't think any of us really realize all that is involved when we decide to have children. However, I must say it is by far one of the most rewarding experiences I have ever had. It is a thankless 24-7 job that requires our blood, sweat, and tears. An adult goes from the "free" life to instantly being responsible for keeping a tiny baby alive. Life goes from selfish to selfless. I'm not saying this to promote negativity or martyrdom; it's just the truth. I was a little shocked at how different life was when I had kids, and I quickly realized I was going to need God to help me every single day to be patient, kind, and gentle and to serve my children. Each day was a huge lesson in dying to myself and learning to yield myself to the serving and nurturing of my children.

In the early years when I stayed home with my children, I learned that if I didn't get up and have quiet time with the Lord, I would not be equipped or have the patience and endurance to really parent them. The preschool years are some of the most demanding times in parenting because our children are still so very dependent on us for everything. Each stage and phase of child development has its challenges for parents, but birth to age five or six years of age is especially demanding.

One of my weaknesses is that I can be inconsistent. I love spontaneity and changing the routines up. Early in my walk with the Lord, I was not strong at having consistent quiet times. I have really invited the Lord to help me develop in this area, and now it is my most treasured time of the day.

God's Book contains so much valuable information, but the advice I think most important for you to receive and apply is that it is critical you get up earlier than your children to start your day fellowshipping with the Lord in solitude. With Him and His power, strength, wisdom, patience, and love flowing in you, you will not fall short of being all God has called you to be as a parent. He will comfort you, refresh you, and guide you in ways no person or program ever will.

"I love those who love me, and those who seek me diligently shall find me" (Proverbs 8:17 NKJV); "Seek ye first the kingdom of God, and his righteousness; and all these things shall be added unto you" (Matthew 6:33 KJV). I believe that literally means we are to seek Him at the beginning of every day, first thing. We are to keep first things first when it comes to our time, our talents, and our treasure (or money).

"Seek the Lord and his strength; seek his presence continually!" (1 Chronicles 16:11 ESV). We all know there will be days when our quiet time just doesn't happen or gets interrupted. This is when we simply pray through the day in bite-size time segments. (Don't condemn yourself because you didn't get your time alone with God.)

By establishing this habit consistently, you will see yourself yield increasingly to the Holy Spirit's leading during your day and receive His help in staying in peace and joy and love and being patient with your children.

Another reward to having daily quiet time is that your children see you modeling prayer and reading

SEEK 1st THE Kingdom

God's Word daily, and at an early age, they will learn how to keep "first things first" in their lives as well.

> And they gathered it every morning, every man according to his eating: and when the sun waxed hot, it melted.
> **EXODUS 16:21 KJV**

> When did the Israelites gather manna? Exodus 16:21 shows that they had to gather their daily bread *first* thing in the morning, before the sun got hot, or their opportunity literally melted away. God's bread is best gathered early in the day, when we first arise, when we and the manna are at its freshest. This sounds like "seek *first* the kingdom of God . . ."! Sometimes, we intend to study later in the day, or in the evening, and what happens? Other things interfere and crowd out the Word of God—and an opportunity to show God He has first place in our life simply melts away, just like manna allowed to sit in the heat of the sun.
> **FORERUNNER COMMENTARY, FROM EXODUS 16:21[1]**

As parents, we need to teach our children by example to help them learn this habit. We need to teach them that the best time to study and pray is right after waking up. Ask them to make their beds and immediately talk to and worship their Father in heaven. If your children are too small to read, then praying over breakfast and reading to them for a few minutes is a good place to start. As your kids get older and their reading capacity increases, make sure to keep quiet time and devotionals concise to help develop a habit that is life giving instead of an obligation.

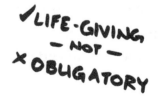
✓ LIFE-GIVING
— NOT —
✗ OBLIGATORY

---

1   *Forerunner Commentary*, "Exodus 16:21," BibleTools.org, accessed June 9, 2019, https://www.bibletools.org/index.cfm/fuseaction/Bible.show/sVerseID/1969/eVerseID/1969.

None of this works unless we ourselves get up in time to put God first, and that will not happen unless we go to bed early enough! To show God we are serious about putting Him first in our lives, perhaps we need to quit doing the things that eat up our time. *God will not just slide into first place. We must consciously put Him there.* We must make this decision every day of our lives.

I saw considerable fruit in my life when I did this. When I got up early to fill up my tank, so to speak, with the love and power of God, I was fueled for the day to handle all the little mishaps and interruptions that come with having small children. This was also the case when, years later, I was working outside the home and had an equally demanding lifestyle.

The most important relationship in your life is not with your spouse or kids but with God. Our lives are intended to be centered on God and His Word. Without keeping things centered, our world, including our relationships, can get out of balance. Time with God refreshes and restores us to be effective in our purpose.

Devotionals are available for every season of life and on different topics. I have listed some of my favorite books for devotions or quiet time for parents in the Digging Deeper section below. You can find many more amazing devotionals in bookstores and online, so take some time to find one that really interests you.

Take a Step

Determine what time of day will work best for you to get time with God. This will probably require modifying what you're currently doing to make it happen. You will probably need to start going to bed earlier to wake up earlier. You will need to prepare a place for your quiet time—a comfy chair, perhaps—and your Bible and journal and maybe a nice cup of coffee or tea. Resolve in your mind that your quiet time with God is the most important part of your day, and you will naturally prioritize it. God gives us our daily bread. We need it every day to live in victory over any chaos and negative thinking that comes our way.

Lean In

Father, you are my first love. I long to be with you more than anything and anyone. I am committing to focus on you first. I want to give you my best and first moments of each day. I know that in your presence is fullness of joy and you desire to give me what I need to thrive every day. I am excited to grow more with you and hear from you. In Jesus's name, amen.

Digging Deeper

- *Sparkling Gems 1* and *Sparkling Gems 2* by Rick Renner
- *The Circle Maker* and *Draw the Circle* by Mark Batterson
- *Jesus Calling* by Sarah Young
- *Brave Girls* by Jennifer Gerelds and Tama Fortner
- *The Authority of the Believer* by Kenneth E. Hagin
- *Being Led by the Spirit* by Kenneth E. Hagin
- *Faith* by Kenneth E. Hagin

> "Wrinkles are hereditary, parents get them from their children."
>
> **DORIS DAY**

Notes

Date Nights

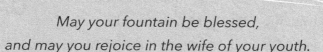

May your fountain be blessed,
and may you rejoice in the wife of your youth.
PROVERBS 5:18 NIV

Study after study has been done over the years that shows the major way kids feel secure and safe is when they see their parents loving each other. This ranks higher than even parents expressing their love directly to their child (although, of course, that is critical also).

When life gets busy with kids and work and schedules, it is easy to place priority on everything *but* your marriage. However, if the foundation of the home—the marriage—isn't strong, then everything else is on shaky ground too. For everything in the home unit to function properly, spending time with your spouse must be at the top of the priority list. If you think about it, everything about your family stems from your marriage. Your marriage is the foundation of the family and it must be protected and cultivated. Naturally, the elements of your relationship change through the years, but the passion that first drew you to each other can grow even stronger through dating your spouse. Date nights are one way to keep first things first. Plus, date nights are fun—it's a win-win situation!

While our kids still lived at home, Mike and I were committed to consistent date nights. Our goal was to have two date nights a month (but more were always good too). We had to have this time together to maintain a deeper level of communication between us and to rekindle any romance that had fallen between the cracks of a busy week. We could also use some of this time to discuss our battle plan to keep the kids from taking over!

Date nights should be about you and your spouse and enjoying your time together. It is natural for some talk about parenting to slip in; however, keep in mind that this time should be focused on your relationship and not be consumed with talk about the kids. It might be healthy to make a rule that on date nights you don't discuss finances, extended family drama, or anything else that could cause friction or fighting. Save those conversations for a separate time. When you find you need time away from your kids to discuss those issues that tend to get emotional or heated, set aside another time to tackle them. Maybe make a standing lunch date once a month to touch on budgeting plans and other heavier topics. Keep date nights light and fun.

NO "SHOP TALK" ON DATES!

Dating your spouse does not have to be expensive—or cost any money at all. Pack a picnic lunch or dinner and a blanket or chairs and go to a beautiful park. Look online to see if there are any free festivals or concerts happening in your town. Just riding around in the car and talking can be incredibly refreshing at the end of a long week. Even more simple than those, leaving a love note or a love text lets your husband know you are thinking of him and still desire to have a romantic relationship with him. Jimmy Evans, author of *Marriage on the Rock,* teaches that it is very important for couples to get away together for a few days from time to time. It might seem like an impossible feat to arrange childcare, finances, and schedules, but it is vital.

Another benefit of date nights (or date weekends, when you can arrange them) is they solidify to your children that your marriage comes before them. Your marriage must be a priority every day. This is not unkind. You will not hurt your kids' feelings. Children have an innate desire for boundaries and order. If they respond negatively to your date nights or weekends, then perhaps they are experiencing the growing pains of not getting all of everyone's attention. That's healthy for them! Spending even a few minutes of quality time—just Mike and me—each day after the kids were asleep helped keep our marriage a priority.

I know I didn't always make Mike feel like he was a priority over the children. Looking back, I could have done a better job of that. I would get so absorbed with the kids and their activities, the upkeep of the house, being with my friends and their kids some, and later working outside the home that he often felt like he wasn't a daily priority. It wasn't an intentional thing. I didn't mean to make him feel that way, but at times I was tired and had nothing to give him. In the season of life when I was home with the kids, I often struggled with my self-worth. The Lord was also dealing with me—He was showing me areas where I was selfish, and so in processing all that, Mike often felt left out.

Be open with your husband about your feelings. Let him know you want to keep him your main priority and that you're trying to figure out how that works in your chosen lifestyle. Work together to keep the passion alive by finding out what he needs and desires at this point in life. God has blessed your marriage, and covenant love is amazing.

We know love isn't a feeling but a choice. You *choose* to stay in love with your spouse. If certain things are trying to hold you back from actively pursuing your spouse or if you have found yourself feeling "out of love," go to God and make your mind up that you will fight for your relationship. And that's when covenant love goes to work! Love isn't a feeling, but the amazing thing about covenant love is that you actually can feel strong passion and love, and it can grow.

Take a Step

If you are not having regular date nights with your spouse, start by scheduling one a month. Book a babysitter in advance and make a plan. If your budget doesn't allow for a paid sitter, ask a trusted family member or friend to babysit. Or better yet, trade babysitting with people. When our kids were little, we would trade weekends with Mike's sister and brother-in-law. We would take their kids for one evening, and they would take ours for another evening—or occasionally for an entire day and night so we would have more than just a few hours on a date or for a discussion time.

Another easy, inexpensive way to date your spouse is to write a sweet love note and put it in your spouse's car to read first thing in the morning. Or one night after your kids have gone to bed, surprise your spouse with a movie night on the couch with their favorite snacks.

Lean In

Father, I am so thankful for my spouse. I know that what you have put together no man can separate. I also know you have blessed our covenant, and I will fight to keep our marriage my first priority. I declare that our marriage keeps getting better and better and that we grow together in new ways. Help me to be attentive to my spouse's needs and desires. I want to keep the passion alive in our marriage, and I thank you for showing me exactly what to do.

Digging Deeper

· *Marriage on the Rock* by Jimmy Evans
· *The Meaning of Marriage* by Timothy Keller

"According to my child,
the perfect amount of time to stay at
the park is five more minutes."

Notes

More Notes

Savor the Moments

> *Time is the most valuable thing a man can spend.*
> **THEOPHRASTUS**

Time is a very funny thing—it keeps moving every second, and it stops for no man (well, maybe one—Joshua). I am amazed that it seems as though it's only been ten minutes since they were five years old, yet now my children are raising their children. People would say things like "Enjoy them while you can; it goes really fast." I would smile and agree, and it felt like I *was* enjoying every minute with them. I honestly felt as if I was able to enjoy each phase and stage without looking ahead to the next season or saying, "Well, when they are _____ age it will get better or easier." But this thing called parenting really does go so fast.

When Sarah and Shaun were younger, I was mindful of creating special events—and daily occasions—they would always remember. (I share some of those in the "Celebrate the Moment" chapter.) Birthdays were always special in our house. The kids got to pick what they wanted to do, what they wanted to eat, and what type of cake they wanted. They could have their friends join them. Pinterest has tons of great ideas for parties these days.

When Sarah was three or four, we had a circus-themed birthday party. It was quite simple, but when she was older, I asked her what her favorite birthday party was, and this was her top pick. We asked the guests to dress up as their favorite circus performers, we ate clown cupcakes, and we had popcorn and peanuts just like what you would buy at the circus. We used the garden hose to make three big rings where the kids performed different tricks I had set up for them to do. We had circus music playing, and I took lots of pictures. We all had great fun.

One of Shaun's favorite birthday parties was a paintball-war party with his friends, which was held in the foothills close to where we were living at the time. I was surprised and amazed at how much those paintballs hurt when you were hit with one, and why anyone would deliberately do this for fun. It's got to be a guy thing!

On Shaun's sixteenth birthday, Mike had some of his and Shaun's closest friends' dads come over to provide some words of wisdom as he approached becoming a man. Mike asked each man to bring something for Shaun that would symbolize his encouraging word. Mike gave Shaun an arrow, and he spoke of releasing him like an arrow toward the path God had destined him for. We recorded it so Shaun could go back and watch it when he wanted.

Sometimes at dinnertime I would read to the family while we ate. One of our favorite books was about a family of missionaries close to the Amazon. This was a great time together and sparked tremendous conversation.

In our house, Sunday nights were family nights. Before the night was over, we would pray together for a few minutes and share with each other what the Lord was showing us. This weekly tradition built much unity in our family and helped us grow together and with God.

Throughout our children's preschool and elementary years, we spent a lot of vacation time going to Oklahoma to visit my aunts, uncles, and cousins. My Aunt Helen and Uncle Lewis lived out in the country and had a swimming pool plus a fabulous pond area, which was excellent for fishing. Since we lived in New Mexico, which has very few lakes and not a lot of water, this was marvelous. The guys would fish some, and Shaun would spend most of his time down by the water exploring and wandering around, finding bugs or insects and other treasures.

As parents, we want to savor and celebrate the big occasions as well as the daily moments. I once read about being intentional to have one-on-one time with each child, where each parent spends alone time with a child a few times a week, or daily when possible. This time is for you to devote a few minutes a day, or as much time as you can, to listening and talking to each one of your children. Set up a time to just focus on them and hear about their day and things going on in their world. That can be done at home or on a date time with your child—go get ice cream or take a walk together or talk when you tuck them in for bed at night. Some of planning a one-on-one time is to pick a time when your child is the most open to talk. It was sometimes a challenge, but Mike and I would do our best to have a few minutes each day to spend time alone with each child. We were savoring the daily moments.

CELEBRATE THE *Big* & SAVOR THE *Small*

Take a Step

Mentally reflect on what time of the day your children are most receptive to talking and telling you about their day and all the things they are feeling or thinking. If it is right before bed, make sure you allow a few extra minutes for one-on-one time with them to really connect with and listen to them. This will help you to know how to pray for them.

Lean In

Father, I am so thankful for Your joy that is my strength. I know I can be content with all things, but because you are so awesome, you have given us joy and happiness to celebrate life. I want to help make meaningful moments special for my kids, but most of all, I want my kids to recognize you are the reason we celebrate and you are the source of our joy. We love our times together and being connected to each other and to you.

"I don't need a big fancy trip. I would be happy with a trip to the bathroom by myself."

Notes

Teach Your Kids to Pray

Be persistent and devoted to prayer,
being alert and focused in your prayer life
with an attitude of thanksgiving.
COLOSSIANS 4:2 AMP

One of the most important things we can do as parents is teach our children the value of prayer in their lives. As they see us regularly praying, they will understand this to be a high priority and of great importance and value. Our words are very impactful, but it is what they see us doing that they will imitate.

You can start teaching your children to pray as soon as they begin to talk. After all, prayer is talking and then listening, just like you would do in any conversation. It is talking to the Creator of the universe, our heavenly Father, about anything and everything, big and small.

I love *The Message* translation of Philippians 4:6–7, which says, "Don't fret or worry. Instead of worrying, pray. Let petitions and praises shape your worries into prayers, letting God know your concerns. Before you know it, a sense of God's wholeness, everything coming together for good, will come and settle you down."

As parents, our job is to prepare our children to be independent, leave our home one day, and live successfully dependent on God the Father. We will not always be with our children in their day-to-day lives, but God is the one who will never leave us or forsake us (Hebrews 13:5).

We started praying with our children at mealtimes and at bedtime. Start with teaching them to say just a few words like "Thank you, God, for our food, in Jesus's name" or "Thank you, God, for a good night's sleep." "The Lord gives me, his beloved, sweet sleep" (Psalm 127:2). As they get older, these prayers can be expanded some to include friends, family members, and other people as well as activities. If we ever saw an accident when we were driving, I would say, "Let's take a minute and pray for the people involved in this accident." We would pray for God to help the people involved and to give them peace. We also wanted to teach our kids to be aware of situations and people around us so we could pray for them at any moment throughout the day.

Opportunities arise every day to make mention of people in prayer. "[I] cease not to give thanks for you, making mention of you in my prayers" (Ephesians 1:16 KJV). From a young age, kids develop pure, innocent love for the people around them. You can capitalize on that by encouraging them to pray for the people in their world. You can do this at bedtime and throughout the day in a very natural way. As children enter elementary school, they can be taught to take the first five minutes of the day to pray and talk with the Lord about the upcoming events of the day or reflect on the day's history.

By middle school, those prayer moments can be expanded more and more. The key is to start a prayer habit with them at a very young age so it becomes the foundation of everything they do.

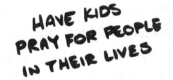

HAVE KIDS PRAY FOR PEOPLE IN THEIR LIVES

Your children will learn to pray as they pray with you. Blogger Dollie Freeman at *Joy in the Home*, in her article "How to Teach Toddlers and Preschoolers to Pray," says, "Children are born with faith. They believe in everything that is told them and they do it with their whole hearts."[1]

Another great place to start prayer is to have your children pray by thanking God for their food, clothing, home, and family. You can teach them to pray for healing by praying over their hurts, pain,

PRAY:
✔ **FORGIVENESS**
✔ **THANKFULNESS**
✔ **HEALING**

and sicknesses. Teach them to pray for forgiveness by helping them to pray when they have been disobedient to God's rules or yours. They can also pray for someone who has hurt their feelings. They can pray for their friends and families or other people. The Bible tells us to "pray without ceasing" (I Thessalonians 5:17). We need to teach our kids to pray anytime and that prayer does not have to be a formal, scheduled event. God loves to hear from His kids all day every day!

Take a Step

Make it a point to start developing small prayer habits with your children. This week, cushion an extra five minutes in your morning schedule to have your kids pray about their day. It is so important to teach our kids to pray according to what God's Word says. As you are teaching your kids to pray, you can also tie in what God's promises say pertaining any matters at hand. Children's prayers will usually be tied to their feelings or their friend's or family's feelings or situations. From an early age, you can help to engrave the living, powerful Word of God on the tablets of their hearts, and as they pray, they will learn to use the Scriptures as fuel for their prayers.

---

1   Dollie Freeman, "How to Teach Toddlers and Preschoolers to Pray," *Joy in the Home*, accessed June 9, 2019, https://www.joyinthehome.com/how-to-teach-toddlers-and-preschoolers-to-pray/.

Lean In

Father, I know the power of prayer. I want my kids to love to pray like I love to pray. Help me to be sensitive to the promptings of the Holy Spirit for great times to pray with my kids. I know the soil of their hearts is good and ready to receive the seed. I declare they are good ground and grow in your ways, God. Thank you for being present and with us at all times. I am captivated by you and love to be in your presence. I pray my kids' desire is to walk and talk with you, even at an early age. In Jesus's name, amen.

Digging Deeper

· *His Mighty Warrior: A Treasure Map from Your King* by Sheri Rose Shepherd (boys)
· *His Little Princess: Treasured Letters from Your King* by Sheri Rose Shepherd
· *Jesus Calling: 365 Devotions for Kids* by Sarah Young
· *I Will Follow Jesus Bible Storybook* by Judah and Chelsea Smith
· Joy in the Home (blog) @ www.joyinthehome.com
· "10 Ways to Teach Your Child to Pray" printable, iMOM (blog) @ www.imom.com.

"Parenting is a conglomeration of everything I've never learned."

DAY EIGHT

Technology

In this day and age, we are bombarded with technology and other things that bring constant interruptions and distractions into our lives. We feel pressure to constantly stay connected through checking email, responding to text messages, scrolling through social media, and reading or listening to the news.

Many of us didn't get a cell phone until we were out of school and into our career. Most of us didn't use a computer in our day-to-day living until we were adults. Our cell phones were originally used for convenience and safety. We used computers for writing papers or work only, never for entertainment. Gradually, phones and computers became much more complex in an effort to simplify our lives. Soon our communication, work, entertainment, and overall life business happened on one device. We can now access virtually anything we can imagine, at any time, any day. What formerly took substantial time to acquire now can be at our fingertips in seconds. What once we had spent hours at the library searching for can now be found in practically no time at all. What previously was passed down through generations can now show up on a screen from someone we don't even know.

Technology is now everywhere, and everyone has access. Our children are growing up in a much different, more technologically advanced world than anyone could have ever imagined. Social media has introduced a new level of information, both good and bad, to our lives. There is an endless supply of opinions, advice, entertainment, and information—and also lots of useless stuff.

Technology and all it entails can feel overwhelming and scary, but we have to face reality—it's here to stay. It is just a way of life now, and we have to have it. But we cannot let it be our master. We must be the master over our devices, internet use, and social media accounts. This goes for everyone in our families. Boundaries should be set up and lines must be drawn to ensure the safety and integrity of our lives. We have to do everything in our power to train our kids to wisely use technology and to set hard and fast parameters around their lives.

I could write a whole book on technology and social media, but I will just touch on a few important notes here.

TECHNOLOGY Boundaries ARE A MUST!

Self-Esteem and Comparison

Social media is the highlight reel of someone's life. It's not reality. It is a one-second view of a 24-hour day, and it can be inflated to make life look perfect. The worst part about social media is the sneaky thief it ushers in: comparison. Second Corinthians 10:12 tells us not to compare ourselves with anyone else. When we constantly peruse social media, we are unknowingly planting seeds of comparison by holding our reality up to someone else's highlight reel. It's not healthy, it's not productive, and it's not worth it. (I mention the harm in that in chapter 11). Social media can be amazing for the purposes of staying in touch with distant family and friends and for being inspired to make a delicious meal, read a suggested book, or discover a healthy fitness routine; but as with anything in life, you need to make a plan for your family's social media use.

Side note: if you aren't doing this already, I would highly suggest having a "public spaces" rule for all tech devices in your home. This means iPads, computers, and even cell phones are used in the kitchen, living room, or other family rooms where the user isn't isolated or in private. Also, have your kids charge their phones in your room every night when they go to bed.

KEEP DEVICES
IN PUBLIC SPACES

Time Management

While we don't want to overschedule our lives, there is freedom in being time managed. Psalm 90:12 says we should ask for God to help us number our days, or be wise with our time. This management should absolutely be in place for technology devices. We have to be good stewards of time, and if we're not careful, a ten-minute social media session turns into two wasted hours. Apps and tools are available to monitor your time spent on social media. These would be very helpful for teenagers.

An idea for managing time on devices for children is for them to earn tech minutes. Put together a list of educational tasks, household chores, and the like they can do to earn minutes on their iPad or other device.

Boundaries

If you don't have boundaries set up for yourself and your children for time online, then you should prepare for disaster. This may seem harsh, but it's true. If you do not, then their innocence could be stolen. If you are not strongly involved in your teenager's social media accounts, things could be awakened that are not meant to be stirred until marriage. Most statistics on pornography use say the average age of a child's first exposure to pornography is eleven years old. According to an article published by Net Nanny, "new research from the security technology company Bitdefender, has reported children under the age of 10 now account for 22% of online porn consumption under 18 -years old [sic]."[1] And an NSPCC ChildLine survey concludes that "a tenth of 12 to 13-year-olds fear they are 'addicted' to pornography."[2] Many experts believe this is due to two primary issues: mobile accessibility and desensitization at an early age. Dame Esther Rantzen, founder of ChildLine, said, "We know they are frequently stumbling across porn, often unintentionally, and they are telling us very clearly that this is having a damaging and upsetting effect on them."[3] (I also address this in chapter 22, "The Talk.")

If you and your spouse are not free to look at each other's phone at any time of any day, then you are at risk for many things to come between you and your marriage. Boundaries are not a matter of being nosy and controlling. Boundaries are for protection and living a free, simple life, one not complicated and destroyed by meddling things that aim to steal our attention and affections. If your spouse wants to look at your phone, it should be no big deal. There should be no secrets in a marriage, and if you take offense to your spouse looking at your phone, then you are allowing secrets to kill your relationship. Your attitude should not be "Don't you trust me?" but "What's mine is yours to see."

Technology has become a master, an addiction for many people. Don't let it master you and victimize your marriage and family.

---

1   Kristin MacLaughlin, "The Detrimental Effects of Pornography on Small Children," Net Nanny, December 19, 2017, https://www.netnanny.com/blog/the-detrimental-effects-of-pornography-on-small-children/.

2   Patrick Howse, "'Pornography addiction worry' for tenth of 12 to 13-year-olds," BBC News, March 31, 2015, https://www.bbc.com/news/education-32115162.

3   Howse, "Pornography addiction worry."

Take a Step

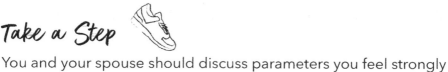

You and your spouse should discuss parameters you feel strongly about putting in place regarding tablets, phones, TV time, and the like. Write down your family's tech plan to include times when devices can be used, how much time everyone has access to devices, and where and when devices are off limits. Also, decide what boundaries you will set regarding *what* each child is permitted to have on their devices. Numerous apps are available that provide tools for parents to monitor their kids' social media and tech usage. Have a family meeting where you discuss the importance of putting a guard over what you see and hear. You can explain that the eyes are the window to the soul, and we must preemptively put up protection over what we take in through our eyes. Make sure to explain to your children how much you love them and that your job on earth is to protect them and help them grow in God. Let them know just how much you want to help them guard their hearts and not be taken advantage of by the tech-savvy world we live in. Be transparent and  real, approaching the conversation from a place of pure, powerful love instead of a place of controlling, forceful, out-of-touch dictatorship. You will likely get some pushback from your kids. That's okay! That's normal! But stand your ground. Keep your tone peaceful and calm and keep your words seasoned with love. Your kids will thank you in the not-too-distant future.

Lean In

Father, I come to you humbly from a position of great desire to protect my children. I place the whole of my care and worry at your feet. I cast it all on you because you care for me and my family. Your Word says to ask for wisdom when I need it, so Father, give me wisdom in the area of technology use in our home. Show me what our boundaries should be and help me to come up with an appropriate plan. I pray for favor with my kids, that your love envelops them as we discuss these details and that supernatural understanding rests on them. I declare that my family will be unified and strong and that we were put on the earth for exactly this moment in time. We are equipped to flourish in today's society, and that is exactly what we will do. Father, above everything else in life, I want to honor you and raise kids who walk closely with you. Thank you for protecting my kids and giving us the knowledge we need to make decisions for our kids. In Jesus's name, amen.

Digging Deeper

· Covenanteyes.com is a website that helps you track any porn-viewing activity on computers in your home.

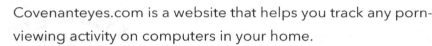

"No smartphones for my kids.
They need to suffer years of fleeting,
awkward eye contact with strangers like I did."

Notes

Let Your Kids Fail

The righteous may fall seven times but still get up.
PROVERBS 24:16 CEB

Most moms can at times be rescuers, but when a behavior continues to happen over and over, and we continue to rescue our kids from whatever situation they are in, we then become enablers. Part of my personality is mercy motivated, which is good unless it is not tempered by the Holy Spirit or balanced. I had a tendency to do for my kids what they could do for themselves and rescued them when they needed to learn the consequences of their own lack of responsibility, misbehavior, or disobedience.

Our son Shaun's personality is all about people and relationships and fun. He is a lot like me. Now there is certainly nothing wrong with that. Some personality inventories call it Sanguine. However, if it is not tempered or balanced with other personality traits, this child could end up being the class entertainer and never learn to read. Ha! We had to work with Shaun a lot on self-discipline and organizational skills.

Frequently Shaun would leave his homework assignments at home. When the kids were in grade school, Mike took them to school, so Shaun would call me to ask if I would bring his homework so he would not get in trouble. I did this several times, but as Mike and I talked about this, he helped me conclude that I was really hindering Shaun by continuing to rescue him. It was really hard on me the next time he called and asked if I would bring him his homework, but Mike and I had already agreed on our plan of action and had told Shaun about it. We were going to allow him to fail as a result of the consequences of his lack of planning. It would probably mean a lower grade, but the grade point wouldn't be as important as the lesson learned. It didn't take him long to start organizing his homework and assignments the night before.

If you are rescuing your children over and over again, you are doing a great disservice to them. It can be something as simple as dropping off homework or more serious as continuing to bail them out of jail. Whatever the case in your home, letting your children fail can be the best thing you do for them.

As your kids get older, they will make mistakes in judgment at times. It is important to listen as they tell you their stories and not rush to bring in condemnation or criticism. Just listen to them. They probably already know what they did wasn't smart at all. Help them figure out what their next step(s) should be and walk them through it, whether it be an apology or restitution. It can be really hard for a parent to see children have to face the consequences for their actions, but it is totally necessary for them to learn and hopefully not repeat.

In her audio book *Teach Your Children Well: Parenting for Authentic Success,* psychologist Madeline Levine says letting kids fail is one of the most critical things parents can do. She asks parents to remember how often toddlers fall when they're learning to walk. That is the  model in life for how kids master things. If we swooped in at the first stumble, a child wouldn't learn how to walk. She walks because she fails over and over again, with our continued encouragement and presence. Levin says learning from mistakes is an important skill, one that helps kids build resilience and mature into confident, happy, and successful adults.[1]

Here are some suggestions from Samantha Parent Walravens to help your children bounce back from failure[2]:

1. Tell your kids that you don't expect them to be perfect. Let them know that your love is unconditional, regardless of whether they get straight As or make the competitive team.
2. Stop rescuing your kids. Encourage them to take responsibility for their mistakes and not blame others.
3. Share with them examples of mistakes you made, the consequences you faced, and how you learned from them.
4. Let them know they are in good company. Point to folks like Michael Jordan and Steve Jobs, who failed before they succeeded.
5. Help your kids see the good side of getting things wrong. Failure can motivate them to practice harder, study longer, or attempt a different solution to a problem.
6. Praise your kids for their efforts and courage to overcome setbacks. Encourage them to try again if they fail the first time.

Not that I have already attained or am already perfected; but I press on that I may lay hold of that for which Christ Jesus has also laid hold of me. Brethren, I do not count myself to have apprehended; but one thing I do, forgetting those things which are behind and reaching forward to those things which are ahead.

---

1   Madeline Levine PhD, *Teach Your Children Well: Parenting for Authentic Success* (New York: HarperAudio, 2012)

2   Samantha Parent Walravens, "Why We Should Let Our Kids Fail," ModernMom, accessed June 9, 2019, https://www.modernmom.com/690ff96c-4e3e-11e3-b437-bc764e0546c6.html.

I press toward the goal for the prize of the upward call of God in Christ Jesus.

PHILIPPIANS 3:12-14 NKJV

I'm not saying that I have this all together, that I have it made. But I am well on my way, reaching out for Christ, who has so wondrously reached out for me. Friends, don't get me wrong: By no means do I count myself an expert in all of this, but I've got my eye on the goal, where God is beckoning us onward—to Jesus. I'm off and running, and I'm not turning back.

PHILIPPIANS 3:12-14 MSG

Take a Step

What are you doing for your kids that they should be doing for themselves? Are there any ways you could be enabling your kids to continue in unhealthy or negative habits? Are you allowing certain behaviors to avoid conflict? How can you show your kids you love them while still letting them learn and grow, sometimes the hard way?

Lean In

Father, I want my kids to be *all* you created them to be. I want them to fulfill the plans and purposes you have for them, and I don't want to stand in the way by allowing or fostering negative behaviors. Show me, by your Spirit, how I can help them grow and learn, and how I can be a strong, safe haven for them without feeding the flame of bad habits. In Jesus's name, amen.

Digging Deeper

- *Teach Your Children Well: Parenting for Authentic Success* by Madeline Levine PhD
- "Why We Should Let Our Kids Fail" by Samantha Parent Walravens @ www.modernmom.com.

> *"I love cleaning up messes I didn't make. So I became a mom."*

Notes

More Notes

Manners Are a Must

> *Do to others as you would have them do to you.*
> **LUKE 6:31 NIV**

Supreme Court Justice Clarence Thomas said, "Good manners will open doors that the best education cannot." Yishan Wong said, "My own father explained it to me thusly, that, 'politeness is the social lubricant between strangers.'"[1]

At the heart of good manners is a respect for oneself and others. Good manners convey a sense of respect for the sensibilities of other people. When you say "thank you," you're taking the time to make the other person feel appreciated. Saying "please" respects a person's right not do what you've asked (it's not so demanding with a "please" attached).

Good manners also show that a child listens to his parents and does what he is taught – these are good character traits that teachers and other authority figures appreciate. . . .

You do your children such a big favor when you teach them good manners. From bosses to girlfriends, good manners can make or break an opportunity. For instance, if your child is up for his first job

---

1   Quoted in "Why is it important to teach children manners?" Yishan Wong, Quora, December 21, 2010, https://www.quora.com/Why-is-it-important-to-teach-children-manners.

and his credentials match another candidate's, the more polite and mannerly candidate may end up with the job. . . .

Simply put, your child may be more successful in life in general if he has good manners.

PAM MYERS, "THE IMPORTANCE OF TEACHING MANNERS TO KIDS"[2]

I like what Kirsten Wilkins has to say too.

Manners are a [sic] outworking of more important heart issues that we teach our children. If we miss the heart issues, saying 'please' and 'thank you' can soon become a somewhat mechanical response for our little ones. Being grateful results in a 'thank you'. Being respectful prompts an 'excuse me'. Being remorseful leads to 'sorry'. If we discipline our children for not having manners its [sic] important to take the time to explain these heart issues to set them up for getting it right the next time.

KIRSTEN WILKINS, "WHY IS IT IMPORTANT TO TEACH CHILDREN MANNERS"[3]

Let's face it, polite children are going to be treated better by other people. By teaching and expecting our children to use their manners, we are giving them tools to help them not only succeed in life but to put into practice the heart of the gospel—to love and respect people.

THE HEART OF The Gospel is Love & Respect

The key to teaching your children manners is to help them

---

2   Pam Myers, BSEd, "The Importance of Teaching Manners to Kids," Child Development Institute, August 17, 2011, https://childdevelopmentinfo.com/parenting/the-importance-of-teaching-manners-to-kids/.

3   Quoted in "Why is it important to teach children manners?" Kirsten Wilkins.

understand why they are using them. We started with "please," "thank you," "I'm sorry," and "excuse me" when they were toddlers. As they got older, we taught them how to respond when they were introduced to new people. We taught our kids to say hello, look the other person straight in the eyes, and answer any questions. We also taught our kids to say "Yes, ma'am" or "Yes, sir." They learned how to answer the phone properly and take messages. That really doesn't apply as much now because so many people no longer have landlines. But even if they answer your phone by first or second grade, they should be saying, "Hello, this is _____. How can I help you?" or "Hello, this is Mom's phone, and I'm _____. How can I help you?"

When our kids were teenagers, we occasionally took them to very nice restaurants so they could experience fine dining with multiple utensils and several-course meals. It was fun to see how they reacted when the waiter put the napkin in their lap. We even used a finger bowl at the end of a meal. Our goal was for them to feel as comfortable in a formal environment as they did on a mission trip.

Etiquette and manners seem to be getting less and less important as society is trending toward a more informal and casual vibe; however, well-mannered kids will be set apart by their behavior and respect. We want our children to be known for their generous spirits and love. One way to help them operate in thanksgiving is to call or send a note to say thank you when they are given a gift. Also, when they are invited to a party, help them to understand the importance of responding in the requested RSVP time. Before Shaun took his first weeklong trip to a friend's cabin, we rehearsed guest etiquette. We talked about being aware of the family culture and being sensitive to offer to help set the table or load the dishwasher, keep his clothes together, and follow the house rules.

American culture is very different than most cultures around the world. Each country on the earth has its own set of cultural norms and acceptable behaviors. After they graduated high school, both Sarah and Shaun took mission trips on their own without us. We talked to them about following some of the cultural customs they might see and, especially, to be a help to the leaders.

A lot of the learning and training of manners happens as things come up along the way. We can always remind our children that all of us learn from our mistakes but manners are about treating others with respect.

Take a Step

Write out a basic code of manners you desire to see your kids follow, as well as societal or cultural norms. Go over these with your kids. If you haven't already, explain to your children how using manners makes others feel honored, respected, and loved. Talk about our purpose to love others and how to show the love of God to everyone we come into contact with. You can create a "manners reward jar" and put in a piece of paper with that child's name on it when you observe his or her use of good manners so they can choose a small reward.

Lean In

Father, thank you so much for loving us. It is our goal to raise kids who love others and honor people. I declare that my children walk in the fullness of your love to such a great measure that it overflows to others around them. I know the deep, pure love for others will motivate them to honor others as well. In Jesus's name, amen.

Digging Deeper

· *365 Manners Kids Should Know: Games, Activities, and Other Fun Ways to Help Children and Teens Learn Etiquette* by Sheryl Eberly

> *"The other night I ate at a real nice family restaurant. Every table had an argument going."*
>
> **GEORGE CARLIN**

Notes

More Notes

Favorites Are a No-No

God does not show favoritism.
ROMANS 2:11 NIV

One of the worst things you can do as a parent is play favorites. We see an example of this in Genesis and the negative results: "Now Israel loved Joseph more than any of his other sons, because he had been born to him in his old age; and he made an ornate robe for him. When his brothers saw that their father loved him more than any of them, *they hated him* and could not speak a kind word to him" (Genesis 37:3-4 NIV, emphasis mine).

The child who receives the blessing may be insensitive to the pain of the unblessed. The unblessed sibling will struggle with *rejection and jealousy.* One sure way to bring division and strife into your home is to show favoritism to one child over the others. We see what happened to the hearts of Joseph's siblings and how Joseph ended up in a pit. That's some pretty big division! We know God redeemed all the years Joseph spent in prison and promoted Joseph, but division was born into Jacob's household because of favoritism. When Joseph's dad favored him so much more above his brothers, it ruined Joseph's relationship with his brothers. It got so very bad that his brothers lied about his death and sold him to merchants. The pain Joseph went through for many years was because his father showed favoritism.

We also see what happened when Rebekah and Isaac played favorites:

> Isaac preferred Esau and his "manly pursuits," while Rebekah favored Jacob, who is described as "a mild man, dwelling in tents." . . . This favoritism put the couple at odds on at least one score, who would inherit the patriarchy after Isaac's death. . . . However, like Sarah before her, Rebekah took matters into her own hands rather than allowing God to work matters out so Jacob would receive the blessing in a more ethical way. . . . We can learn lessons from what actually happened—lessons about the use of trickery, favoritism in families, getting ahead of God, making assumptions about what He is doing, priorities, selfish ambition, parental manipulation of their children, how one lie begets another, and so forth. We can mine a wealth of wisdom from the rivalry of Jacob and Esau.
>
> **RICHARD T. RITENBAUGH, *FORERUNNER COMMENTARY* ON GENESIS 27:16[1]**

These are very dramatic stories of how favoritism devastated and brought division to some very prominent families in the Bible.

One way we might show favoritism toward our children and not even realize it is when we let our youngest child do things our older children didn't get to do, or allow them to get away with not doing things we required of our other children. I saw this in myself when I read James Dobson's book *The Birth Order.* I noticed I tended to do things for my son that at his age I wasn't doing anymore for our daughter, our firstborn. Sometimes we think, *This is our last child, so*

---

1   Richard T. Ritenbaugh, *Forerunner Commentary* on Genesis 27:16, BibleTools.org, accessed June 9, 2019, https://www.bibletools.org/index.cfm/fuseaction/Bible.show/sVerseID/744/eVerseID/744.

it's okay that I just do this for them rather than require they do what they can do at the age they are.

Another very important no-no for parents is to compare your children to one another. The Word of God says we are not to compare ourselves among ourselves. "We do not dare to classify or compare ourselves with some who commend themselves. When they measure themselves by themselves and compare themselves with themselves, they are not wise" (2 Corinthians 10:12 NIV).

Each of our children is different and has been created by God with diverse talents, abilities, and giftings. I think it is insulting to our children if we expect one to achieve the very same things the other one did. I cringe when I hear parents say, "Well, your brother never did this," or "Your sister got straight As." The more a parent does this, the more it creates a breeding ground for jealousy, inferiority, and insecurity in your children. A certain amount of rivalry occurs between siblings for the parents' approval and attention anyway, but constant comparison is destructive to their self-esteem. It's like saying, "You just don't rate up to your brother/sister."

I address in Chapter 1 more on how we want to instill in our children a spirit of excellence, not perfectionism. We want our children to do their best, and if that is a C, so be it, or if it's an A, so be it too. What we need to monitor in our children is that they are putting the time in to learn what they are supposed to be learning both scholastically and in character development.

The only F I ever got in school was in seventh grade Home Economics class for my conduct because I talked all the time, didn't pay attention to the assignment, and I prevented other girls from finishing their sewing or cooking assignments. I was horrified Mrs. Thompson would actually give little ol' me an F in conduct. I had to explain the reason to my parents. They didn't tell me my brother had never received an F, but they did tell me I had to apologize to Mrs. Thompson and cut out the talking and horsing around. I did apologize, and that grade came way up, but I didn't have my parents comparing me to anyone else.

As parents, we will love each child in a different way, because each child is unique and different.

Take a Step

Take a few minutes to step back and look at your relationship with each of your children. Have you unknowingly favored a certain child? It is natural and normal to have an easier connection with one of your kids based on similar interests and personalities you may have. However, we must be ever conscious to ensure we don't use that to connect more with that child and have less of a connection with our other kids. Our relationship with one of our kids might be easy and natural, while our relationship with our other kid(s) might be much more difficult and require a lot more effort, but it's worth the effort!

Work to find something you have in common with each child, or just notice your kids for who they are as individuals. We can have amazing relationships with each of our kids, even the ones who are harder for us to understand.

It helps to understand what your kids' love languages and personality types are. When you know those things, you can better love your children in the way they most easily receive love.

Lean In

Father, I thank you for your love and for loving each of us, your kids, uniquely. I receive your love and accept your power to help me to love like you—without filters, judgment, or preference. Show me how to see my kids the way you do and to love them as they are. Also, help me to develop deep, meaningful connections with each of my kids. I know you have specifically appointed and equipped me to be the parent my kids need. I am so thankful for my children and declare that this is the start of new things in the relationships I have with my kids. In Jesus's name, amen.

Digging Deeper

- *The Birth Order Book,* James Dobson
- "Bible Verses about Parents Playing Favorites (From Forerunner Commentary)," Richard T. Ritenbaugh, (https://www.bibletools. org/index.cfm/fuseaction/Topical.show/RTD/CGG/ID/17776/ Parents-Playing-Favorites.htm).

"You're a parent when it takes longer to get everyone in the car than it does to run the errand."

Notes

More Notes

Is Your Love Unconditional?

> *Though I speak with the tongues of men
> and of angels, but have not love, I have become
> sounding brass or a clanging cymbal.*
> **1 CORINTHIANS 13:1 NKJV**

Your first response to this chapter is probably going to be a resounding *yes,* but some things we parents do and say affect how our children perceive whether we love them. Unconditional love is best modeled to us in the life and death of Jesus Christ. Before we ever knew about Him, He loved us. His love for us is unconditional and is totally based on His character and goodness, not ours.

The society we live in today puts a priority on performance. It rewards performance, usually above all else. We see a generation of professional kids—kids whose parents have put them in music, tech, or sports lessons at a very early age. Sometimes they are in a different lesson each day of the week. Some parents want their kids to be Olympians by fifth grade. Children today are under tremendous pressure to perform—and perform well. Long gone are the days when kids just got to play when they got home from school.

There is nothing wrong with wanting our children to excel in the areas they are gifted in, but the new trend is an extreme exaggeration of this. We want our children to do well and achieve and win, but how do we handle it when they do poorly, make mistakes, or just plain fail at something? Everything is usually based on winning, but how well do we prepare our children to lose graciously?

For many years when I was a kid, I was on the swim team. At one particular meet, I had competed in several events, but the 50-yard backstroke stands out because of how devastated and embarrassed I felt. It was the last event of the meet, and I was in last place. I mean *really, really* last, and so far behind that when I got to the finish line at the end of the pool, everyone else swimming in the event had left the area. I felt so embarrassed and discouraged. But my mom met me in the locker room, and she immediately spoke words of encouragement to me as I cried. I knew she and my dad loved me very much. More importantly, I knew they loved me whether I came in first place or last place. I felt their unconditional love for me even when I (in my own eyes) was a loser.

It is also crucial that our children see and understand that their parents love them even when their actions are inappropriate and their behavior disobedient. They will have to realize there are consequences to disobedience or inappropriate actions, but they need to know our love for them remains constant, just like our heavenly Father's love remains constant for us. We can convey to them that whether in first place or last, our love for them never changes. This is one of the greatest gifts we can give our children.

Every child goes through failures, mistakes, and disappointments. The key is their knowing they are *not* a failure, a mistake, or a disappointment and that you will love them unconditionally their entire lives.

Another thing I had to guard against was not letting pride affect how I viewed any mistakes or misbehavior the kids displayed. Kids are learning and growing; they will make mistakes and do or

Love REMAINS *Constant* ALWAYS

say things that embarrass us, but that is part of the process. When we allow their behavior to affect our self-esteem or self-worth, we are yielding to pride and conditional love.

He presented himself for this sacrificial death when we were far too weak and rebellious to do anything to get ourselves ready. And even if we hadn't been so weak, we wouldn't have known what to do anyway. We can understand someone dying for a person worth dying for, and we can understand how someone good and noble could inspire us to selfless sacrifice. But God put his love on the line for us by offering his Son in sacrificial death while we were of no use whatever to him.

ROMANS 5:6-8 MSG

That's called unconditional love.

Take a Step

Look at the dynamics in your home, and take the temperature, so to speak. Is it an atmosphere of love and acceptance? Can you identify an area lacking love? Can you be assured your kids know you love them no matter what? Have you told them this?

Don't wait any longer to let your children know about your unconditional love. Invest into making sure they know what unconditional love is. Don't stop there; make sure you communicate your love multiple times daily.

Lean In

Father, your love is all-encompassing, never ending, and committed. Your love carries and strengthens me. I will draw on your everlasting love to pour into my own children. I want more than anything for my kids to know and comprehend your great love at an early age, and I know a large part of that comes through my love for them. Help me to see by the eye of faith, not filtering my affection through frustration or anger but through love. In Jesus's name, amen.

Digging Deeper

· *How to Really Love Your Child* by D. Ross Campbell, M.D.

"Motherhood: Powered by love, fueled by coffee."

Notes

Do You "Get" Your Kids?

> *Train up a child in the way he should go [and in keeping with his individual gift or bent], and when he is old he will not depart from it.*
>
> **PROVERBS 22:6 AMP**

One of the most important things about being a parent is being able to identify and understand different personality types. This is a skill we need with people throughout life, but it starts in our own homes. As an only child for the first seven years of my life, it was a regular routine for me to sing, dance, do tricks, and put on shows for my mom and dad and others. I was a very friendly and outgoing child and loved talking to anyone. I have continued to be outgoing and friendly throughout my life.

When Sarah was about four, her preschool class was performing a few songs in the Christmas program. I was totally shocked and dismayed when she began crying before the class was to go on stage, not wanting to sing. I kept wondering what was wrong with her. Mike simply pointed out she obviously didn't want to do that. To me that was unbelievable because who in the world would not want to perform for other people?

Soon I began to notice other ways Sarah and I were very different, which was quite puzzling because I thought she would be just like me.

It was becoming more obvious she wasn't! This began my quest to figure out what was going on. As I started researching information on personality types, I gained insight from many perspectives and studies. The DiSC profile and the Myers-Briggs Type Indicator, along with many other personality tests, can help you understand your own personality traits as well as your child's.

The study I am most familiar with is from the research by Hippocrates that laid the foundation nearly 2,500 years ago for the personality profiling studies we have today. It is based on blood types.

There are four basic personality types, and all of us are a blend of one to two of these types. Here is a general overview of them, from Florence Littauer's book *Personality Plus:*[1]

1. **Choleric** –Born leader, goal orientated, outspoken, competitive, strong-willed.
2. **Sanguine** –Life of the party, sociable, talkative, makes friends easily, imaginative.
3. **Melancholy** –Perfectionist, analytical, deep and thoughtful, respectful, sensitive.
4. **Phlegmatic** –Sympathetic, peaceful, calm, patient, easygoing.

You can find many simple questionnaires online to figure out your child's personality type, some of which I mention in the Digging Deeper section below.

The main point is that it is important for all parents to truly understand their children's personalities. It is a big mistake to think they will automatically be just like us or another sibling. As I studied, I really started to "get" how Sarah was wired. She is a Melancholy-Choleric personality rather than a Sanguine-Phlegmatic type like me and her brother. She was a little more introverted when she was younger, and she likes things very organized. In high school she would draw a line down the bathroom mirror so our son Shaun wouldn't get

---

1   Florence Littauer, *Personality Plus* (Grand Rapids: Revell, 1992), 24–27.

water spots on her side of it. Even in grade school, she didn't like her brother sitting on her bed because he might get the bedspread dirty. They are very opposite in many ways. As they got older, I would tell them they would probably marry someone like their brother or sister because usually opposites attract—so they'd better learn to get along and compromise some. That thought always made them shudder! Ha! Actually, I was pretty much right on in so many ways.

Of the four personality types and blends, one is not better than the others. They all have their strengths and weaknesses. As Mike and I began to understand the personality traits more, we could better understand our kids and help them in their weaker areas. With Shaun, we had to focus on helping him with

his organizational skills and habits. He was the class entertainer and the life of every party, but he needed help in organizing his time and study. Sarah, on the other hand, was disappointed if she even got an A-, so we had to work with her about not being such a perfectionist all the time and to lighten up a bit and have fun. One time we planned to take the kids skiing on a Friday as a reward for such good attendance at school, and we wanted to have a family day. Shaun had no trouble at all with that idea; however, Sarah had to be reassured repeatedly that it would be okay to miss school just this once. Quite ironic, since the reward was for good attendance!

The key is to understand the differences in all our personalities and how we perceive things and to allow the Holy Spirit to help us to be well balanced and not extreme. When we are tempered and well balanced, we operate in traits of all four personalities, and we help our children do that also. You and your spouse should take some personality profiling tests too. If you have very young children, you can still see some of their personality basics being developed in their lives.

Take a Step

Research and find a couple of personality tests you, your spouse, and your children can take. Make sure to read the thorough descriptions of each personality, the strengths and weaknesses, and other details. As a family, discuss each personality and give examples of how each person thinks, feels love, and lives. By working as a family unit to better understand each other, you will create a strong family bond. At the same time, you will be helping your children learn about people who are different than they are. They will gain vital skills for listening to understand, and communicating successfully, with people who think differently than they do.

Lean In

Father, thank you for creating each person in our family with specific, unique characteristics to be used for your kingdom and to love others. Open the eyes of our understanding to better know and appreciate your design in each person and help us to really hear each other. We want to be a strong family unit who loves others and doesn't judge just because we are different than someone else. You are an amazing God. Thank you for using us to grow your kingdom. In Jesus's name, amen.

Digging Deeper

- *Personality* Plus by Florence Littauer
- *Delight in your Child's Design* by Laurie Winslow Sargent
- *Raising an Original* by Julie Lyles Carr. The book contains a questionnaire for your kids to answer. Carr makes some noteworthy points about not parenting by fear and ensuring we are discovering and nurturing the unique personality traits in our children.

· *The Road Back to You* by Ian Morgan Cron and Suzanne Stabile. It is based on a number system of helping you determine your personality traits.

"Children scream and fuss when it is time to go to bed...teens scream and fuss when it's time to wake up!"

Notes

More Notes

DAY FOURTEEN

Are You Having Fun?

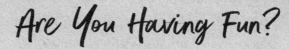

A merry heart does good, like medicine.
PROVERBS 17:22 NKJV

I am a firm believer that your home should be like a little piece of heaven on earth. There are several elements that create a heavenly home, but one major factor is fun. If kids can have fun with their family, it naturally creates a strong, positive bond between the members of the family, and the kids will want to be around more. They will enjoy being at home rather than want to escape to their friends' homes or other places. When kids have fun with their family, they feel safe and secure. When kids can laugh with their parents, they desire to be around them and feel confident in that relationship.

I have a Sanguine personality, so fun is just built into who I am. I know that's not the case for all personalities—fun doesn't come easily for every type—but if you tend to be a more serious or quieter person, you can still initiate and incorporate fun into your family! Even if your family is going through a tough time, you can still have fun. In fact, it would be monumental for your kids to learn at an early age how to be joyful in all things and find fun, even on dark days. It teaches your kids that no matter what the family faces, when we put our trust in God, we don't have to worry and can enjoy life. You can cultivate an environment of fun, no matter what!

While our kids were growing up, each weekend I tried to plan one fun activity I knew the kids would enjoy. It would range from a family bike ride, a walk, or a trip to the park together to going to get ice cream, playing tennis, or bowling.

What does your family like to do? What kinds of activities have you enjoyed on your vacations? Is one of your kids more introverted and interested in doing calm, less active things? Is another one into sports? Do you or your spouse have a hobby? If you are having trouble coming up with fun activities, have a family meeting and ask each family member to write down a few activities they love to do that the whole family could do. Put each person's responses into a jar, and each weekend pull a paper out to see what the fun family activity will be. Some ideas for staying in are movie nights with pizza, family game night, or a puzzle night with fun snacks. Going out can include attending a play or visiting a museum, learning to paint a picture together, going on a hike and having a picnic, or catching a sporting event.

The bottom line is, think of a way to show interest in things your kids are interested in, but help them get out of their comfort zones by doing new things. Family fun does not have to be expensive. In fact, you don't have to spend any money. Unconventional ideas can be enjoyable too! Have a coloring contest with your teenagers. Think outside the box and build an environment in which your kids feel confident being silly, laughing, and enjoying

FAMILY FUN $ CAN BE INEXPENSIVE!

the differences in family members. When your kids laugh together, it builds a subliminal bond that turns into friendship. Your kids can actually end up being the best of friends.

Once we had some family friends staying with us for a weekend. Mike went out and jumped on the trampoline with the kids, and since it was summertime, they had the hose out and were spraying each other. Everyone was laughing and having a good time. One of our friends said to me, "Your family has so much fun together." The way she said it made me think that wasn't necessarily the case in her family. I believe God is right in the middle of love and laughter, and we know He loves families. He wants us to enjoy life together. When our families are happy and delighting in life, it brings glory and honor to God: "Then our mouth was filled with laughter and our tongue with shouts of joy; then they said among the nations, 'The Lord has done great things for them'" (Psalm 126:2 ESV).

God loves when we enjoy ♡ each other

Another way to build an environment of fun in your home is to encourage your kids to invite their friends over. If your kids are taking pleasure in their family, then it is natural they would want to invite their friends to join in the fun. It's a way of bringing their two worlds together. We loved when our kids' friends would come to our house and just hang out. One reason for this is that we could monitor the music they listened to, the movies they watched, and the activities they were involved in. We have to be conscientious enough to let our kids be kids while still guiding them and being present. What better way to stay in touch with our kids and their interests than to see how they are with their friends? Also, this gives you a bird's-eye view into who your kids are hanging out with. One of the most critical things we do as parents is make sure our kids are around the right people: "Do not be deceived: Evil company corrupts good habits" (1 Corinthians 15:33 NKJV).

"A merry heart does good, like a medicine, but a broken spirit dries the bones" (Proverbs 17:22 NKJV). The Message Bible says it this way: "A cheerful disposition is good for your health; gloom and doom leave you bone-tired." We should be willing to laugh at ourselves and teach our kids to not take themselves so seriously, even when they make mistakes. We don't have to be perfect or have perfect kids. We are dependent on God and His Word to help us trust Him daily in everything we do.

I believe laughter happens during fun, carefree events, but it also comes from within. Our attitude needs to be cheerful and positive, and that emanates from the things we think about on a regular basis. It is a privilege to be a parent, and it is a huge responsibility we are entrusted with by our heavenly Father.

However, while I do have a natural inclination toward fun, I think there has to be a balance in our lives between spirit, soul, and body. We should set aside time to pray and read God's Word, individually as well as together as a family. We need a fixed time for work and keeping our home in order as well as occasions to play and have fun.

Physical activity should also be part of our lives—as parents and in our children's lives as well. And eating healthy food builds into our children's habits for a lifetime.

DON'T FORGET ABOUT Physical Activity

Exposing your children to a variety of activities and experiences enables them to better decide what they might want to be involved in or study. For example, we tried to expose our children to cultural arts events like seeing ballets, musicals, and concerts.

I encourage you to make sure you have a balanced atmosphere in your home with activities that involve fun and laughter as well as work and discipline. "Summing it all up, friends, I'd say you'll do best by filling your minds and meditating on things true, noble, reputable, authentic, compelling, gracious—the best, not the worst; the beautiful, not the ugly; things to praise, not things to curse" (Philippians 4:8 MSG). Let this verse inspire you to cultivate an environment of fun in your home by focusing on how good God is and that He wants us to enjoy life!

Take a Step

Make a Family Fun Jar by having each member of your family submit three or four ideas for a fun family night. Schedule a night, at least once a month but preferably more often, for family fun, and draw a suggestion from the jar. Keep in mind that family fun does not have to cost any money! It might also be a good idea to let your kids invite a friend to family fun night every once in a while.

Lean In

Father, thank you so much for being a fun God! I know you want me and my family to enjoy life, as you have paid a great price for us to be free to laugh and smile. When we enjoy life, it is a witness to others about how much joy and happiness we have in you. As we plan fun moments for our family, I invite you to direct and lead us. I know you will be in our midst as we are gathered together, so I ask you to unify us as a family under your banner over us, which is love. I declare that as for me and my household, we will serve the Lord. I pray that in these family nights, each of us will experience real, true joy and laughter and that it is good, like medicine, for us. We love you so much. In Jesus's name, amen.

"Before having a kid, you must ask yourself: Am I ready to watch the same cartoon on repeat for the next four years?"

Notes

Childhood Hurts

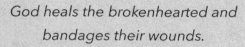

God heals the brokenhearted and
bandages their wounds.

PSALM 147:3 CEB

My childhood was filled with love and laughter and lots of family time. I knew that my parents loved me deeply and I was wanted. My mother married her childhood sweetheart. He had a history of heart problems, though, and after only six months of marriage, he died. Soon after that, my mom moved in with her sister and brother-in-law and their children. She loved her nieces and nephews and desired to have children of her own. She met my dad, and they got married in 1948. They had me pretty quickly, and seven years later, my brother, Dean, was born.

My parents weren't perfect, of course, but they loved each other and were very affectionate toward one another. They genuinely loved my brother and me and showed their affection to us as we were growing up. My husband was also raised in a very loving family. We both grew up hearing words of love and receiving healthy physical displays of affection from our families. Their examples and actions carried over to our marriage and family.

Does this description of my family seem totally foreign to you? You might have had a totally opposite experience. Perhaps you lived through abuse, divorce, abandonment, or substance abuse. You are not alone. Through thirty-plus years in ministry, I have come to realize that the childhood I experienced is not the norm. We have personally ministered to hundreds of people who have had incredibly negative childhood experiences. The devastating truth is that more people than not have personal heartbreaking stories of childhood abuse, neglect, and trauma.

If you are a survivor of childhood trauma, I am so sorry for the horrors you have lived through. I am here to tell you there is healing and hope for you today. The Word of God says the enemy comes to steal, kill, and destroy, but Jesus came that we would have life and life more abundantly (John 10:10). Satan wants to take the abuse and trauma of our past and use it to keep us in bondage to destructive behaviors that will 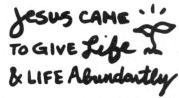 eventually destroy us physically, mentally, socially, and spiritually; but you don't have to live another day in bondage to your past. Not only that, your childhood does not have to negatively influence the way you parent. You are not your parents. Regardless of your childhood, it is more than possible for you to have a peaceful, happy, and safe family and home.

There are some negative outward signs of the inward trauma you may have lived through that need to be dealt with for the sake of your children. One big symptom that can affect the way you treat your family is hurtful words. If you find yourself regularly berating your children with words like "Why can't you do anything right?" "You are bad, very bad," "Why can't you be like your sister or (brother)?" or "You are so dumb," you need to take a step back and examine why you say these things. Is there frustration in your life you are taking out on your children, or are you just modeling and repeating what you have experienced as a child from your parents? We know words can be just as damaging to our children as physical or sexual abuse. Many people have said our words are containers of power. "Death and life are in the power of the tongue, and those who love it will eat its fruit" (Proverbs 18:21 NKJV).

If you find yourself acting out in negative ways toward your children, the first step in getting help to break destructive cycles is to recognize there is a problem. The next step is to ask the Lord to help you overcome any negative parenting behavior you have found yourself practicing. "God heals the brokenhearted and bandages their wounds" (Psalm 147:3 CEB). It has long been said that hurting people hurt people. God wants you whole and healed and free from the pain of childhood hurts you may have, and free from repeating negative parenting habits you were raised with.

Two books I highly recommend and believe will help you go through this journey to healing are listed in the Digging Deeper section. With these, you devote daily time to reflect on and answer questions that will give you great insight into hurts and wounds from the past that you haven't dealt with or settled—a few of the topics are: discovering self-esteem, recognizing compulsive behavior, release from shame, overcoming the fear of joy, hurt for people who grew up too soon, perfectionism and procrastination, and healing painful memories.

SPECIAL NOTE: We know the healing and restorative power of God is real. We have seen marriages and families that seemed utterly hopeless be completely healed and refreshed. While we reference a couple of books we find to be very helpful, we also fully believe in Christian counseling and encourage you to seek out this service if you feel led to do so. Christian counselors are licensed and trained to provide clinical tools to help you. Getting help when you need it is wise and brave.

Take a Step

If you would like to:

- ✔ identify and understand problems and feelings from your childhood tha t might be affecting your parenting skills negatively,

- ✔ identify ways your past is affecting your future negatively,

- ✔ unlock buried feelings from the past and experience healing and forgiveness, and

- ✔ help remove emotional, psychological, and spiritual barriers to better fellowship with God and others,

take a few minutes to pray and see if ordering *Making Peace with Your Past* and completing the workbook can help you gain insights and freedom in those above-mentioned areas.

Lean In

Thank you, Father, for helping me be the best parent you have called me to be. I ask for your help to recognize behaviors in myself that might not be healthy to me or to my children, and I ask that you would give me the power to overcome them. Your Word tells me that "I can do all things through Christ who strengthens me" (Philippians 4:13 NKJV), and I thank you in advance for helping me to recognize and change any unhealthy or nonproductive behaviors in my life.

Digging Deeper

These are books I recommend for helping with childhood hurts and wounds:

- *Shadow Boxing* by Dr. Henry Malone
- *Making Peace with Your Past* and *Moving Beyond Your Past* by Tim Sledge. The *Making Peace* books are workbooks.

> *"The trouble with being a parent is that by the time you are experienced, you are unemployed."*
>
> **UNKNOWN**

Notes

More Notes

Are You in the Rhythm?

> *I can do all things through Christ who strengthens me.*
> **PHILIPPIANS 4:13 NKJV**

Do you feel the rhythm? Are you wondering what in the world *the rhythm* could be?

It has become normal for families to be outrageously busy and on the go all the time. Because we are used to fast-track living, we go through the minutia of everything that must get done every day without recognizing how out of balance the different areas of our lives can get. We juggle work, school, sports, homework, extracurricular activities, and social obligations, and before we know it, we haven't spent time with God in two weeks and can't remember the last time we exercised or went on a date with our spouse.

I found myself in this whirlwind over twenty years ago. We were in the very early years of starting our church, and I was trying to balance ministry life, my full-time job as a teacher, and most importantly, raising our two teenagers. I am so thankful I came across a book called *The Rhythm of Life: Putting Life's Priorities in Perspective*. This book impacted me deeply when I was in the middle of a chaotic time needing balance.

One of the greatest treasures we can give our children is to show them how to live a well-balanced life. Richard Exley writes that to be in the rhythm of life that "God has planned for each and every one of us to live in, we need to master the balance of work, rest, worship, and play."[1]

Parenting is hard work; it's the hardest work. Most of the time we feel completely spent before the day is even over. According to Exley, it doesn't have to be that way. He says, "Life doesn't have to be a rat race. I believe all of that can be turned around. I believe work can be meaningful, rest can renew, worship can inspire, and play can be the joyous pleasure that seasons it all."[2] Take a minute and just think about that. Are you practicing the rhythm of life—enjoying that delicate balance between work and rest, worship and play? Are you fulfilled? Are the most important relationships in your life all they should be? Do you take time for yourself? for God? What about play? Are you fun to live with?

I will give you a brief recap of the four essential lifestyle practices to keep your life in balance as a person and as a parent.

Work

God created us with a desire to work. Work is healthy and makes us feel productive. However, if we aren't intentional in keeping this part of our life in balance, it can be destructive to our health and to our family life and other relationships. It's easy to be driven to achieve what we consider success. We see it as providing for our family and creating a better future, even though it often keeps us away from our children and we miss out on making memories. When Mike and I started the church, our kids were about to finish high school and leave for college. It started becoming a habit for both of us to stay late at work, skip

Family is your Priority

---

1   Richard Exley, *The Rhythm of Life* (Tulsa, OK: Honor Books, 1987), 15.

2   Exley, 73.

eating together, and put in way too many hours at the church. We were not living a balanced life. Work at church began to come before our relationship with our kids. Thank heavens the Lord started to show us where we were out of balance, and we got our priorities back in order.

Rest

Do you find yourself thinking, *Yeah, some rest would be nice, but it's utterly impossible right now*? Perhaps you are a parent of young children or have a new baby, or maybe your kids are older and more self-sufficient so you have taken on more work at the office. Regardless of your situation, do you feel like finding time for rest is impossible, even laughable? There are seasons of life that feel overwhelmingly exhausting. You are not alone.

Ask God to help you find time to rest. He is eager to help you and will provide answers. Maybe it's forcing yourself to take a thirty-minute rest during your baby's morning nap, or perhaps it's initiating a mandatory rest time for all your kids at the same time every day. Discuss your needs with your spouse and work together to find a time when he can take the kids out for a fun afternoon so you can take a nap. Rest is critical for us to be healthy, happy, and alert to make good decisions. Rest is not a common habit in our culture that thrives on being busy, but that is not wise nor something to be proud of. We are most effective as parents when our bodies are healthy and strong and have the proper rest.

When I was in my twenties and my children were little, I started a habit I still practice daily: I took a fifteen-minute power nap while they were napping. I still take power naps today. I wake up refreshed and ready to finish out the day. This is just how my body functions best. Another way I incorporate rest into my routine is sometime during the weekend I will take at least half a day to lie on the bed and read the

POWER NAPS FOR THE WIN!

Word or another book and just be still. This practice has helped me to be balanced and more prepared for the expected and unexpected events that happen in life. I love the way Richard Exley says it: "Without the Sabbath, without rest and renewal, without the love of family, I would never have the resources to reach out to a hurting world. Rather than isolating us, the Sabbath renews us so we can effectively involve ourselves in a broken world."[3] The Sabbath, or practice of rest, refreshes us so we can be effective and at the top of our game as we parent our children.

Worship

Mr. Exley also so beautifully explains that worship "enables us to forget ourselves for a while. It's the only cure for our deadly self-centeredness."[4] When we take time daily to worship our Creator, to have hearts full of gratefulness and to be able to express that to Him—whether in song, thought, or conversation—we tap into a relationship that is supernatural, alive, and vibrant. Our relationship with God, through Jesus Christ and by the power of the Holy Spirit, is what keeps us fully alive spiritually and living the abundant life.

Worship does not have to be a formal ceremony. Worship does not have to be forced. Worship is a natural response to the incredible promises of God and the fact that He paid such a great price for us. Praise and thanksgiving are the secret weapons to breakthrough. Thanking God for who He is and what He has done is something we can do all day every day. When we stay thankful in a place of worship, we are refreshed at a supernatural level—spirit, soul, and body.

PRAISE & THANKSGIVING ARE YOUR WEAPONS

---

3 Exley, 80.

4 Exley, 107.

Exley says:

Rest restores our physical vitality and renews our emotional energies. In restful solitude, we forget the world with its pressing demands for a while and remember who we are. Worship goes a step further and enables us to forget ourselves for a while and remember who God is. It puts everything into perspective. In worship we remember the goodness and the greatness of God. Against this backdrop, life's most disconcerting difficulties become somehow manageable. Or as the apostle said, "If God is for us, who can be against us?" (Rom 8:31).[5]

Play

The final element in the rhythm of life is play. Another thing I learned from Exley is that "play relieves the tension and gives balance to the whole of life. By divine design, we need it all, and we ignore this rhythm at our own peril. Without it, the hardiest among us risk burnout. Life's richness hangs by a slender thread."[6]

=PLAY= *enriches* OUR LIVES

My husband, Mike, loves to be outdoors and work in the garden. When he was growing up, he spent some summers on his aunt and uncle's farm with wide open land all around him, and he still enjoys being outside working with his hands. For him, play is gardening. Because of his green thumb, each year we have amazing tomatoes and a variety of flowers that bloom in all seasons. He also recently bought a motorcycle and enjoys riding the open road.

I'm a little different than Mike. Exercise is my playtime. I don't love it right when I start, but once I get going, it is very therapeutic.

---

5   Exley, 107.

6   Exley, 107.

Paul Thigpen, author of *Dad, Are We Having Fun Yet?*, says:

Real play, as opposed to work masquerading as play, is characterized by self-forgetfulness and an absorption in the activity at hand. Work concentrates on goals, achievements and turning out products. It's focused on the future. But play is centered on the present; on the joy of a process pleasurable in itself. When our "play" becomes chiefly concerned with winning, keeping rules, or reaching some "educational" objective, it's no longer play. *When motivation is something besides fun, it's work.*[7]

When I exercise, I am able to let go of the incessant thoughts about my life or others and just be in the moment. I also love to go on bike rides, swing with my grandkids, and swim in the summer. I don't think there is anything that makes me feel more childlike and carefree than being active. Going to the park with your kids helps them enjoy the benefits of being active and being in the moment.

Mike and I have brought play into the rhythm of our lives for years, and our kids were able to be a part of it. We regularly had friends and family over to our house for dinner and games or to celebrate holidays together. We took our kids along with us to play tennis, go on hikes, rollerblade, ski, and do a variety of other activities. Participating in activities together as a family is really unifying and fun.

I pray that you see the value of keeping the balance in your life of work, rest, worship, and play. Without each of them, we can fall into a rut of daily going through a routine without the joy and energy of being in His presence. Without operating in His strength, we begin

---

7   Paul Thigpen, quoted in Richard Exley, *Living in Harmony: Moving to a Better Place in Your Life* (Green Forest, AR: New Leaf, 2003), 156.

to feel like parenting is drudgery, and life can seem like fulfilling one obligation after another in an endless cycle of activity. It is really possible to live the John 10:10 abundant life He came to give you.

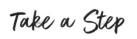

Take a Step

Look at the words listed below. How are you doing in these areas? Next to each word, write down a couple of ways you can bring balance to that area.

Work

Rest

Worship

Play

Lean In

Father, thank you for sending Jesus so I can live an abundant life, no matter what season I'm in. I thank you for your promises that accommodate for every single situation I face. Show me, by your Spirit, ways to bring balance to my life in tangible, applicable ways. I know I can do all things through Christ who strengthens me, and my situation is full of hope.

I declare that our family lives in a healthy rhythm and balance because we are in sync with you. I am so thankful for my family and my spouse. Thank you for equipping me to be an amazing parent who leads my children to you and shows them how to live a healthy, happy, successful, fulfilling, fun life of purpose.

Father, I know you said that the same Spirit that raised Jesus from the dead quickens my mortal body, so I receive that supernatural energy and rest now. Thank you for being a God who delights in us and wants us to live an enjoyable life. I'm excited, God! I trust You! I love you so much. In Jesus's name, amen.

Digging Deeper

· *The Rhythm of Life* by Richard Exley

> "Mother: (noun) One person who does the work of twenty. For free."

Angry Kids

> *A soft answer turns away wrath,*
> *but a harsh word stirs up anger.*
> **PROVERBS 15:1 NKJV**

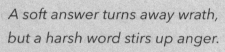

In my over thirty years of ministry, we have received a lot of questions from parents about their kids being angry and about dealing with intense anger issues.

Years ago, as I began the search for resources with the answers to help parents on this topic, I came across a book that has been a goldmine: *The Heart of Anger: Practical Help for Prevention and Cure of Anger in Children* by Lou Priolo. I highly recommend this book. All children get angry from time to time when they don't get their way, but if you feel like your child's heart is full of anger, and angry outbursts are a normal part of his or her daily routine, this book is especially good for you to read and study. I learned so much, and my children didn't even have anger issues.

While the book is full of good points, two really stood out to me. The first was asking ourselves if Mike and I were doing anything to provoke our children to anger. The Bible addresses this directly:

Fathers (moms included though) do not irritate and provoke your children to anger [do not exasperate them to resentment] but rear them [tenderly] in the training and discipline and counsel and admonition of the Lord.

EPHESIANS 6:4 AMPC

Fathers, provoke not your children to anger, lest they be discouraged.

COLOSSIANS 3:21KJV

As I read the book, I learned there are some very specific ways we might provoke our children to anger, and I began to realize how I was inciting or could continue to incite my own children. When I studied the list of ways Priolo explains we can provoke our kids, I discovered I was guilty of many of them. Some surprised me like being inconsistent with discipline, constantly finding fault, comparing one child to another, not making time just to talk, and not keeping your word.[1] He actually lists twenty-five ways, but I just named a few.

I knew in my heart that inconsistent discipline and not keeping my word were things I was guilty of doing because I was not really self-disciplined. I was off-again/on-again with discipline toward Sarah and Shaun. And some days I backed up what I said, while other days I didn't—it could be as simple as telling them we would go to the park that day and then not doing it or saying I was going to cook something and then not making the food.

The Lord began to deal intensely with me about this. He kept impressing me with the fact that I represented Him to my children and if they knew I didn't keep my word or that my word couldn't be depended on, then they would think the same thing about Him, their heavenly Father. That was devastating to me. I knew the Scripture says in Matthew 24:35 (NKJV) that "heaven and earth will pass away, but

---

1   Lou Priolo, *The Heart of Anger* (Amityville, NY: Calvary, 1997), 30–51.

[God's] words will never pass away." His words created everything, and if there was one thing I wanted my children to learn, it was about the power in God's Word. That was a defining moment for me, and I asked the Lord to help me in this area of weakness in my life. I did not desire to provoke my children to anger through this or be a poor representative of God to my children. I received help from above and continue to grow in this to this very day.

During this same time, the Lord began to show Mike that he was provoking the children—in particular, Shaun. Shaun played basketball, and after games Mike would go over all of Shaun's mistakes with him. Mike thought this was being helpful to Shaun, but instead, it was discouraging him. One day the Lord showed Mike that he was Shaun's dad and not his coach and to focus on what he was doing right. That one thing brought much closeness to their relationship.

The second thing that really impacted me was the chapter about a *child-centered home*. I had never heard that term before. This concept is partially based on Proverbs 29:15 (NASB), which says, "The rod and reproof give wisdom, but a child who gets his own way brings shame to his mother," and partially on the widespread acceptance of humanistic philosophy into our culture.[2] Priolo explains:

> [A child-centered home is] one in which a child believes and is allowed to behave as though the entire household, parents, siblings, and even pets exist for one purpose—to please him. A child-centered home is one in which children are allowed to commit the following indiscretions: interrupt adults when they are talking, use manipulation and rebellion to get their way, dictate family schedules, take precedence over the needs of the spouse, demand excessive time and attention from parents to

---

2   Priolo, 199.

the detriment of the other biblical responsibilities of the parents, escape the consequences of the sinful and irresponsible behavior. The list goes on. . . .

The opposite of this is a God-centered home in which the child perceives that the husband is the head of the family and the wife is submissive to her husband. Theirs is  the primary relationship. It is permanent and exists to glorify God. Children have secondary and temporary relationship.[3]

After reading and praying about what we had read, Mike and I made some changes in our home to ensure we were modeling and portraying a God-centered home. This information has not only been invaluable for us personally but has also been a blessing to other families who have desired to get their homes in order and not unknowingly provoke their children to anger.

It is easy for us to feel unheard as parents. We might have to repeat things over and over again before our kids respond. While that's not the expected response from them, it does not mean we should raise our voices or yell. We can easily draw out anger from our kids by creating a tense, mad environment. Our kids will hear our tone and see our actions and then dish it right back to us or their siblings. Remember, they are learning how to behave, respond, and act from us. That is harsh, but it's true. If we are constantly speaking to our children in frustrated, rude, elevated tones, chances are our kids will respond in like manner. They will have no other choice than to explode with the anger bubbling up inside them. We must focus first on our own behavior before we can ever address our kids' behavior.

---

3   Priolo, 24, 28.

The Word of God tells us we will reap what we sow. Let's be conscientious to sow seeds of peace, joy, love, and kindness, and we can expect to receive a harvest in our children.

Take a Step

Pay attention to your communication with your children. Are you drawing them into a fight? Are you using passive-aggressive words that will inspire anger or mean sarcasm? Are you using hurtful words that will provoke your kids to be defensive and hurt?

The Bible tells us our words should be sweet like honey. Make a conscious effort to not be moved by your kids' actions or words. Resolve to respond in peace with a steady, even tone. When kids do not behave, it does not give us the right to withhold love or make them feel any less loved. Our words and tones can and should stay consistent, regardless of what we see and feel. Our kids will begin to return that behavior toward us and will learn self-control at the same time.

Lean In

Thank you, Father, for being so kind and gentle and loving to us. Help me to temper my words and actions with peace and love. I want my kids to know how great you are, and I know they will learn some of that from me. I will let my words be sweet and bring healing to the innermost parts of their hearts, just like your Word says. Help me to stay far, far away from provoking my precious children to anger. I declare that my home is free from strife and that peace and joy and wholeness reign here! In Jesus's name, amen.

Digging Deeper

· *The Heart of Anger: Practical Help for Prevention and Cure of Anger in Children* by Lou Priolo

"88 percent of parenting is saying 'it's bedtime' 150 times between 8:00 and 9:00 every night."

Notes

Talking Heads

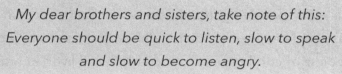

> My dear brothers and sisters, take note of this:
> Everyone should be quick to listen, slow to speak
> and slow to become angry.
>
> **JAMES 1:19 NIV**

When your spouse says, "We need to talk," it can immediately result in feelings of dread or glee, depending on your personality. Some of us are natural-born talkers, very in touch with our feelings. Others of us are less interested in talking, especially about our feelings. Whether we have the gift of gab or the talent of less talk, we all have to realize that *good communication* is not a bad term but something all relationships must have to thrive and be successful.

Even if you are an innate communicator, situations in life can sometimes cause you to be less interested in sharing what's going on inside. Time and trials can create rifts in relationships. Without the proper tools, communication can be twisted into an abusive, hurtful knife that injures a relationship. If you want a happy family, it is absolutely necessary to have healthy communication channels, and that must start at the top—with the parents. The parents then model and teach healthy communication for the kids in that area.

In the book *Crucial Conversations* by Patterson Grenny McMillian and Switzler, a crucial conversation is defined as "a discussion between two or more people where 1) stakes are high, 2) opinions are opposing, and 3) emotions run strong."[1] That is pretty much everyday conversation for a husband and wife with kids! Learning to have these important conversations in marriage and parenting will take some skill to be successful. Planning and scheduling time when everyone involved is not tired is also critical to having a healthy marriage and healthy communication with our children.

Drs. Les and Leslie Parrott, in their book *The Good Fight*, say the top five things couples usually argue or fight about are money, sex, work, parenting, and housework.[2] From my own personal experience, I can vouch for all five of those as being our main points of conflict when our children still lived at home. Now we are down to only four things, haha! In all seriousness, these are big issues that need to be continually addressed and discussed to keep your marriage and family healthy. In hindsight, I can identify one major area Mike was probably very frustrated with early in our marriage, but at the time, we didn't have the right tools for communicating through this area of conflict.

On our dates we would evaluate how we had been doing with our parenting skills and what we saw that needed adjustment and strategy. Sometimes we concluded we were yelling too much or were repeating ourselves. Once we could get a handle on and recognize what we weren't doing or where we were frustrated or what was going on in the family, we could usually figure out what needed to happen next or ways to correct our behavior. Many times when we went out, we would try to find the humor in what was happening with the kids after venting to each other, or we'd laugh at ourselves for how we had responded

1   Kerry Patterson, Joseph Grenny, Ron McMillan, and Al Switzler, *Crucial Conversations: Tools for Talking When Stakes Are High*, 2nd ed. (Singapore: McGraw-Hill, 2012), 2.

2   Drs. Les and Leslie Parrott, *The Good Fight: How Conflict Can Bring You Closer* (Brentwood, TN: Worthy, 2013), 141.

to something they did or didn't do. Finding humor in parenting and marriage is vital. When Mike and I could laugh at ourselves, with each other and in front of Sarah and Shaun, they learned to laugh at themselves too.

Over the course of the forty-seven years we have been married, we have read many books and attended conferences on communication, and we are still learning. These days, many good tools are available. Some of the best communication tools I have learned through the years are 1) active listening, 2) emptying the Emotional Jug, and 3) "you and I" messages.

I write more about "you and I" messages in Day 25 on communication, but I will briefly explain the first two, since you may not familiar be with them.

Active listening is simply repeating to the other person what you think they are saying. By repeating what your husband has said, you are showing empathy for him and are encouraging him to share his feelings, ideas, or concerns rather than just rushing to try to fix him or say what you want to say. First, you give him time and focused attention to say what he wants to, then you can add what you think would benefit him or the situation, or you offer your perspective *if he asks for it.*

Emptying the Emotional Jug[3] is an exercise that will begin to uncork emotions that have been suppressed and not been talked about or dealt with for a long time, if ever. It is excellent as a starter to bring both people to a deeper understanding of each other, but not to necessarily try to bring advice or fix the other person. You start with both people sitting down facing each other in a quiet place. One person, say the wife, shuts her eyes, and the husband begins to ask the following questions:

---

3   "Learning to Listen with Empathy," Purpose Built Families (PAIRS Foundation), accessed July 23, 2019, http://participant.pairs.com/listening_with_empathy.php.

- He might ask, "What are you mad about?" and then gives her time to answer.
- Next he asks, "What else are you mad about?" and he lets her talk.
- Then he says, "If there was anything else you could be mad about, what would it be?" and again gives her time to answer.

He moves to each emotion—sad, scared, glad—without saying anything. He doesn't try to fix or solve a problem; he just listens and lets her get everything out emotionally. Then they swap roles.

You can continue this process as long as is needed. Then it's time to switch roles and ask the other person the questions. Mike and I have done this at times when we're experiencing tension in our relationship and need to get some things out in the open. We might not have been in a place to go any further than to just hear the other person out, go to bed, and revisit the issues a few days later when we weren't upset or angry. My daughter, Sarah, has gone through this exercise with her daughter, Bailey, after she had a trying day at school. Sarah was trying to help Bailey identify what she was feeling so they could pray about some things and take action if needed.

Having effective communication in our marriages will make our foundation much stronger. As a result of a strong marriage foundation, our children feel more secure and loved, and they'll gain healthy communication skills that will benefit them in many areas of life.

Take a Step

Go through the Emotional Jug practice with your spouse and/or one of your children (of any age). Practice active listening and saying back to your child or husband what he has just said to you. Get into the habit of going through life's issues together. Also, put the Emotional Jug into practice when your kids go through hard times and when you are going through a stressful time with your mate or close friend, as well as in times when you just aren't sure what is going on with you internally. It really helps to get through some emotions and feel relieved.

Lean In

Father, I am so thankful for my spouse and children. I ask that you help us to clearly communicate with each other and understand what the other person is feeling. I know you have put us together, but you also know we are different people. Thank you for helping us to be unified and patient with each other. Guide us along this communication path so that our words would be filled with love and peace. In Jesus's name, amen.

Digging Deeper

- *Crucial Conversations*, by Patterson, Grenny, McMillan, and Switzler. This is an excellent book to help parents to communicate with each other and with their children.
- *The Good Fight,* by Doctor Les and Doctor Leslie Parrott. This would be another good book to get and take a chapter at a time to read and discuss together.

"Everyone knows how to raise children except the people who have them."

Notes

Protection for Your Family

> *Put on all the armor that God gives you, so you can defend yourself against the devil's tricks.*
>
> **EPHESIANS 6:11 CEV**

It is crystal clear that we are living in dangerous times. We see evil happening all around us and hear about it on the news every day. For parents, our number one concern is the safety of our children. Fear wants to consume us and dictate how we live our lives. Times have certainly changed, but God and His steadfast promises have not.

I grew up in a time when walking to the grocery store or playing kick the can in the street and hide-and-seek with neighbor kids every night in the summer was commonplace. There was no sense of danger lurking around every corner like there is today, thanks in part to 24-7 media overexposure to horrific scenarios. We absolutely need to be aware of what is happening around us, but we must also put a guard up around what we see and hear. It is vital that we filter everything through the Word of God and rely on God's Spirit to lead us, and on His promises to protect us.

The first time Shaun wanted to ride his bike up to the grocery store, my first reaction was fearfully wanting to yell noooo! But early in our days of parenting, Mike and I made a decision to raise our kids in faith and not fear. The Bible says that as believers we are to "walk by faith, not by sight" (2 Corinthians 5:7 NKJV). *Sight*, in this case, was all the reports we'd seen of children being kidnapped. I decided to let Shaun go. He was with a friend, and we went over important parameters and gave him a time schedule. As he rode down the street, I prayed over him and asked the angels to protect him.

As Sarah and Shaun got older and gained more independence, like spending the night at friends' houses and driving, I began to apply some principles I will share from God's Word that have given me much peace and have protected them to this day. They are both married now and have their own children, and they apply these principles to their children's lives.

The book I read that brought me much **① DISCIPLINE** peace and knowledge from God's Word was Kellie Copeland Kutz's book *Protecting Your Family in Dangerous Times*. She says we can do four things, according to the Word of God, to protect our families in dangerous times. The first step Kutz discusses in protecting your children is to "discipline them."[1]

One of the first Scriptures Sarah and Shaun had to memorize was on obedience: "Children, obey your parents in the Lord for this is right. Honor your father and mother (which is the first commandment with a promise), so that it may be well with you, and that you may live long on the earth" (Ephesians 6:1-3 NASB). When you train and discipline your children to obey you, it is actually bringing *protection* to them. Their obedience can bring long life and make things going well with them. That is because when they begin to obey you, it trains them to obey other things like laws and speed limits that are set up to protect them.

"The second thing we can do to protect our families," according to Swisher, "is to make sure every day that we **② DISCERNMENT** are listening to our spirit and any thoughts

---

1   Kellie Copeland Kutz, *Protecting Your Family in Dangerous Times* (Tulsa, OK: Harrison House, 2002), 9.

or impressions the Lord is wanting us to hear and know."[2] "The spirit of truth will show us things to come" (John 16:13). When we spend time daily in His presence, we are training ourselves to tune into His voice, and He can protect us from what the enemy wants to do in our lives.

"The third way that we can bring protection to our families is by taking advantage of angelic protection."[3] **③ ANGELIC PROTECTION** "Are they not all ministering spirits, sent forth to minister for them who shall be heirs of salvation" (Hebrews 1:14). Born-again believers are the *them* in this verse. On a regular basis, I ask the angels (through God) to take care of and protect my husband, children, and grandchildren. I also ask them to take care of our home and church property and other family members.

"The last source of protection we as believers have is to apply the blood of Jesus over our families by faith. Most believers know the power of the shed blood of Jesus to forgive us of our sins, but they don't know about the **④ BLOOD OF JESUS** protection it provides. One example of this principle is with the Israelites on the night of Passover. The death angel came through the land to kill the firstborn in every household as a sign for Pharaoh to let God's people became free from slavery, but he didn't touch the houses that had blood on their doorposts. Today we don't kill a lamb and place its blood on the doorposts of our homes, but we do apply the blood of Jesus, by faith, around our homes, automobiles, and family members daily with the words we speak."[4]

I have put these principles into practice for over forty years now, and I know they are effective in keeping Satan from bringing harm and destruction into our lives or the lives of our children.

---

2   Kutz, 6.

3   Kutz, 4.

4   Kutz, 3.

Take a Step

Put a guard on what you allow into your home on the TV, radio, and internet. Too much news can be a bad thing and can usher in a spirit of fear. We must proactively counteract the standards of the world by declaring what we will and won't allow in our families. Be offensive in your profession of faith in God's protection, and also on the offensive against fear. God knows what we face every day, and it is not His will for us to be bound in fear. He wants us to be free to enjoy life, and part of this is through confidence in His Word and operating in the wisdom He has for us.

Lean In

Father, I dwell in the secret place of the Most High and I abide in your shadow. I say of you, Lord, you are my refuge and my fortress; my God, in you I trust. I will not fear evil or terror. I will not expect evil. I abide in and expect your protection and safety for my family. I rely on you, Holy Spirit, to lead and guide me into all truth and to tell me about things to come. I am free from fear and am confident in your promise of peace of protection. In Jesus's name, amen.

Digging Deeper

· *Protecting Your Family in Dangerous Times* by Kellie Copeland Kutz
· *The Blood and the Glory* by Billye Brim. If the blood of Jesus is a new concept for you, or you haven't received any Bible teaching on it, I strongly suggest you read this. It covers the subject very thoroughly.
· *How to Be Led by the Spirit* by Kenneth E. Hagin. If you are not familiar with all the teaching about the Holy Spirit, I would recommend reading this.

- *Angels: Knowing Their Purpose, Releasing Their Power,* by Charles Capps. Another excellent book that goes into more detail about this topic of angels.

"Family: A social unit where the father is concerned with parking space, the children with outer space, and the mother with closet space."

EVAN ESAR

Notes

More Notes

DAY TWENTY

Love Languages

> *And over all these virtues put on love,*
> *which binds them all together in perfect unity.*
> **COLOSSIANS 3:14 NIV**

Every child deserves to be loved and nurtured into being all God created him or her to be.

As you know by now, I'm sharing the books that have been so beneficial to Mike and me as we were raising our two children. *The 5 Love Languages of Children* has been a wonderful help.

According to authors Gary Chapman and Ross Campbell, the five love languages are:

1. physical touch,
2. words of affirmation,
3. quality time,
4. gifts, and
5. acts of service.[1]

Their book explains each of the love languages and helps you discover which are your child's. All of us need to learn about each other's love languages as we express our love to others. It might seem difficult to discover your child's main love language until after the age

---

1   Gary Chapman and Ross Campbell, *The 5 Love Languages of Children* (Chicago: Northfield, 2012).

of three or four, and it is important to remember that as your child grows and develops, it might change.

From the beginning of life, all kids need to receive quality time with their parents and lots of physical touch. As they grow older, you begin to see them expressing their love in different, more specific ways. My daughter was in elementary school when we would go over to our good friends Tom and Sheryl's home to play cards, where she would delight in spending a large amount of her time with their daughter cleaning and organizing her room. Shaun would enjoy quality time with their son, playing games or shooting BB guns. Even as young children, it became clear what one of their love languages was: Sarah's was acts of service, and Shaun's, quality time.

I even observe one of my granddaughters at nine years old taking pleasure in giving gifts to us and others. As you begin to recognize what your children's love languages are, you will be better able to connect with them on the level and in the way they need. Everyone receives love in different ways. It is critical for us as parents to be able to clearly decipher and understand the ways our kids receive love. Just because one of your kids receives love in a different way than you or your other kids, that does not make them weird. God wired each of us to have a unique purpose on earth. It just makes sense that we would all give and receive love differently.

YOUR Children HAVE Unique PURPOSES

The 5 Love Languages of Children introduced me to the concept that each of us has an emotional tank. The authors say it so well:

> When your child feels loved, when her emotional tank is full, she will be more responsive to parental guidance in all areas of her life. She will listen without resentment. But there is an equally grand reason to learn your child's love language—and to speak the other four languages as well. As we speak love in the five languages, all

the while specializing in her language of love, we show her how to love others and her own need to learn to speak others' love languages.[2]

As we are able to show our children unconditional love and learn to keep our children's emotional love tanks full, they, in turn, will learn how to speak other people's (friends, siblings, spouses) love languages as they grow and develop into adults and be a huge blessing to them. Likewise, they will feel full of genuine, godly love and will be less likely to look for love in the wrong places and ways.

If you don't know your own love language or if you are married and don't know your spouse's, it will be a good thing to take the inventory yourself.

It's interesting to see my grandkids as they are developing their love languages. I've seen them operate in gift giving and acts of service as well as in words of affirmation and physical touch.

The sad truth is that few children feel unconditionally loved and cared for. And yet, it is also true that most parents deeply love their children. Why this terrible contradiction? The main reason is that few parents know how to transfer their heartfelt love to the hearts of their children. Some parents assume that because they love their children, the children automatically know this. Other parents think that simply telling a child "I love you" will sufficiently transmit that love. Unfortunately, this is not true.[3]

Let's be parents who know how to communicate and connect with our children in the language they most need to hear it in.

Enough said.

---

2   Chapman and Campbell, 105.

3   Chapman and Campbell, 25.

Take a Step

Have you ever taken the Love Languages test? It is so interesting and enlightening to identify our love languages. Not only will this help your marriage, but it will also help your whole family. If we can really love our kids the way they perceive and receive love, our relationship with them is much more secure. Go to this site to help your kids take the love languages test today! http://www.5lovelanguages.com/profile/children

Lean In

Father, I am so thankful for my family. What an amazing idea you had to create families. I want to love and understand my kids for who they are. Help me love as you love us—divinely and specifically. More than that, I declare that even as young children, my kids know your great love and receive it freely. I pray they grasp the height and width and depth of your love for them and abide in that love every day. In Jesus's name, amen.

Digging Deeper

· *The 5 Love Languages of Children* by Gary Chapman and Ross Campbell.

· Teens Quiz: https://www.5lovelanguages.com/discovery-ages-teen/

· Couples Quiz: https://www.5lovelanguages.com/profile/couples/

"Happiness is having a large, loving, caring, close-knit family in another city."

GEORGE BURNS

Scheduling

> *I have said these things to you,*
> *that in me you may have peace.*
>
> **JOHN 16:33 ESV**

After our first child, Sarah, was born, I began to realize how important it was for me to be organized and for our home to be in order. I tend to be a rather spontaneous, free spirit and was beginning to sense the need for greater discipline and self-control in my life. I had been a teacher for five years, but when Sarah was born, we made the decision that I would stay at home with our children. This was a very big step of faith for Mike and I because we were accustomed to living on two incomes.

Sarah was a great sleeper and pretty consistent in taking at least two naps a day. I quickly realized any errands I needed to run had to be done between her nap times. Just like I had a schedule when I worked outside the home, I needed to get a realistic schedule for our home, where my children could take their normal naps and I could still do the things I needed to do.

The Word of God talks about managing our own households: "For if someone does not know how to manage his own household, how will he care for God's church?" (1 Timothy 3:5 ESV). I don't think this Scripture only applies to ministers but to every believer. We as believers are to manage our households in several ways. One way is the management of the natural side of things—keeping things organized and clean, having a system for paperwork in place, and having schedules current. The other type of management, I believe, has to do with managing our relationship with the individuals in our home—learning how to actively listen to one another, resolve conflicts, and set boundaries and rules.

When my children were in preschool, they had a schedule that was different than when they started elementary school. I had to once again adapt our plans to what worked best for their schedule. We had to eat early in the evening so they could help with setting the table and doing the dishes. We ate dinner together and talked about the day's activities and events. After dinner they made their lunches for the next day and worked on homework. If either of them had any incidents or conflicts that had happened during the day, we talked about how to handle them in the future or the next day. Sometimes I would read a book aloud for about fifteen minutes, but after dinner was the one time we could all be together and regroup after each day's activities.

For all this to happen smoothly, I had to have menus and grocery lists. I needed to be wise in managing my time so everything would run smoothly and the kids would get to bed consistently at the same time each night.

Sleep is one of the most important things for our kids. According to the National Sleep Foundation, if your kids are six to thirteen years old, they need nine to eleven hours of sleep every night.[1] But studies have shown that kids today are getting less sleep than kids did thirty years ago. This is in large part because kids are busier these days. They participate in

DON'T FORGET ABOUT SLEEP

---

1   National Sleep Foundation, "How Much Sleep Do Babies and Kids Need?" accessed June 12, 2019, https://www.sleepfoundation.org/excessive-sleepiness/support/how-much-sleep-do-babies-and-kids-need.

sports at an earlier age, and things like school events, music lessons, and tutoring, for example, add extra hours into the evening. When kids get home, they have homework, eat dinner, and if possible, spend time with the family.

Scheduling will seem like a no-brainer for personality types that are naturally well organized, but for someone like me, who had to learn the importance of scheduling and then begin doing it, it will take more effort. If you get your kids on a schedule as babies, it will be easier to incorporate scheduling as they get older. Keeping a schedule will also help your kids learn time-management skills as they get older.

A big note here is to understand that while sticking to a schedule is critical to maintaining good balance in the home, it is also vital to recognize there will be days when a schedule flies out the window. That is okay! Relax! Keeping balance and order is important, but kids are kids, and sometimes things don't go as planned. Your kids will see how you adapt to changes, and it will show them how to be flexible and stable no matter what. Make sure to stay in a place of peace. In each situation, peace doesn't mean nothing is going on, it just means you are not flustered or anxious amid the activity or events that come out of nowhere. Whether the schedule works or doesn't work, stay in peace. If you find yourself consistently lacking peace or feeling chaotic, this might be a sign something needs to be modified. Ask the Holy Spirit to show you where you can rein things in or let things go. He is faithful to lead and guide you into all truth and tell you of things to come (John 16:13).

Take a Step

Every Saturday or Sunday, when there isn't a lot going on, sit down with your spouse and a great cup of coffee and discuss everything scheduled for the next week. Write down practices, appointments, assignments, dinner times, and so on. This is a great time to plan meals and make your grocery list. When you are both on the same page about schedules, you can work together to carry the weight of the busy week. Moreover, discussing schedules in a calm, peaceful moment will help set the stage for a peaceful week. Your brain will take in the details and process them all in tranquility. Make sure to include moments of downtime or rest in your schedule, maybe even include a fun date with your spouse!

Lean In

Father, thank you for the opportunity for my kids to be involved in the activities they are in. I know many kids don't get to do extracurricular activities, and I am so grateful my kids have that opportunity. I cast my cares on you about the upcoming week and scheduling. Help me to stay in a place of peace, no matter what. I want to reflect to my children that I trust you and can remain steady and calm, regardless of what I face. Help me to make the most of our time. Thank you for giving me the mind of Christ to know what to do in every situation. Also, reveal to me any part of our schedule that is not necessary or beneficial. Thank you for leading me into all truth by your Holy Spirit. I greet this week with excitement and peace because I know you hold our days in your hands! In Jesus's name, amen.

"Parenting is mostly just informing kids how many more minutes they have of something."

DAY TWENTY-TWO

The Talk

> That is why a man leaves his father and mother
> and is united to his wife, and they become one flesh.
> **GENESIS 2:24 NIV**

In Anne Marie Miller's book *5 Things Every Parent Needs to Know about Their Kids and Sex*, she says, "One thing I've learned over my many decades is that having a conversation about the birds and the bees (who came up with that saying, anyway?) is anything but a one-time event. Rather, it is a continual conversation you begin to have with your toddler at the age of two—when your child is starting to learn about parts of the body."[1]

She also states, "It's not very realistic to think that your child will not face temptation and can be sheltered from sexual discussions."[2] It is totally normal to feel a little awkward or uncomfortable as you start to have conversations about sex with your kids, but the more you can talk about this, including letting your kids tell you what their friends are saying about it, and can answer any questions they have, the easier and more natural the conversation can become.

God created our bodies to have and enjoy sex in marriage. We

---

1 Anne Marie Miller, *5 Things Every Parent Needs to Know about Their Kids and Sex* (Grand Rapids: Baker, 2016), 53.

2 Miller, 93.

don't want to present sex or our bodies in a negative light but rather as a gift to be enjoyed. In fact, Proverbs 5:18 (HCSB) says, "Let your fountain be blessed, and take pleasure in the wife of your youth." However, a huge key in this conversation is to keep it age appropriate.

When I was a kid, my dad was a health educator and had access to many helpful resources. One Saturday when I was in fourth or fifth grade, my mom invited some of my neighborhood girlfriends and their moms over to watch a video my dad provided about how our bodies would be changing, our periods starting, and everything that involved. We all felt very special and in the know about what to expect. My parents always used the proper names for our body parts and explained that no one should see them or touch them but us or our parents or a doctor. I don't remember many other conversations other than those. I do remember knowing sex was for when you were married, but I didn't hear much about keeping out of situations that might lead to premarital sex, especially if you were "going steady" with a boy.

When my kids were younger, Mike and I found a lot of insight from a James Dobson book I believe was titled *Preparing for Adolescence*. When the time came, we talked separately to the kids. We wanted our kids to hear things from us rather than be misinformed from their friends or other sources. As they got older, we discussed what the Bible says about purity and how to avoid situations that could end up leading to actions they would later regret. Second Timothy 2:22 (NKJV) says, "Flee also youthful lusts; but follow righteousness, faith, love, peace with those who call on the Lord out of a pure heart." The church we were attending at the time had a youth group they attended, and the leaders were saying the same things we were saying.

Things have changed so very much since my kids were growing up. Pornography is available everywhere—on our phones, computers, the TV. Kids are exposed to porn or have seen porn by age eight or nine because it is so easily accessible. All a child has to do is type in the words *sex* or *kissing*, and a boatload of information and pictures pop up. Even if your child doesn't have a phone or a computer, chances are their friends or their friend's parents do. We can do many things to protect and shelter our children from porn and pray over them regularly, but at some point in their lives they could be exposed to it.

So what are the best things parents can do to help their children form a healthy view of sexuality?

In addition to fostering an ongoing, open conversation about sexuality, parents can use real-life opportunities to engage in conversations about sexuality, rather than feeling required to deliver a serious talk. For example, if you see something on TV that is sexually unhealthy and not in line with your values, rather than simply changing the station and ignoring it, talk about why it doesn't align with your family's beliefs. Tell your kids what you believe and why it's important. Or if you see one of their friends treating another person in a sexually inappropriate way, take time to talk about why that behavior's not right and what you want for your child.[3]

Your kids will likely forget a one-time talk or might be too embarrassed to really listen to you at first. Instead, use everyday teaching moments to engage in conversation. Those individual conversations will add up to your kids having a much healthier view of sex.

Let your kids know it's natural to be curious about sexuality, and talk to them about it. Use that curiosity to reframe the discussion

LOOK FOR REAL-LIFE OPPORTUNITIES

---

3   Miller, 90.

around sex, emphasizing that it is a beautiful thing God has created. Remind them God has a purpose for sex, which is why we need to set healthy boundaries concerning it. Help kids understand the connection between the beauty of sex and the values you hold as parents and as a family.[4]

We come back to simply saying what God's Word says about sex in marriage. It is a good thing. I've given you several options of age-appropriate books that can help you begin conversations with your child or children in the Digging Deeper section.

It's important to not discourage your child from forming a healthy view of sex by your silence on the subject— that might communicate to your child shame or judgment. You want your children to form a healthy view of sexuality by keeping your communication with them open so they feel  safe talking about things with you. Many children are just curious. They can have questions about the human body or about pictures they may have seen. Don't shame them by discouraging them from talking to you about what they saw or how they felt. Part of our job as parents is to help our kids not awaken habits or desires that need to be kept asleep until they get married.

As our kids got older, I would ask the Holy Spirit to alert me if there were situations or environments that our kids might be getting involved in that could foster an unhealthy sexual situation. If they were going to their friend's houses, I would find out if the parents were going to be home and who would be there. We can't always be with our older kids everywhere, but we can pray and believe that the Word that is in them will be brought to their remembrance in any given situation. Sarah and Shaun both waited until they were married to have

---

4   Miller, 90.

sex, and I know a very big factor in that was them knowing God's Word and having His help and His power to be able to do that.

Take a Step

The best thing you can do to be well prepared for the Big Talk is to access the amazing resources available on the subject. We want our kids to feel like they can talk about anything with us and to consider us their safe place. However, if we aren't prepared for their questions or conversations, they might hesitate to talk to us about it again. Make sure you are willing to calmly discuss anything your kids want to, whether it's related to sex or not. The more they talk to you about other things, the more they will talk to you about the awkward things too.

Lean In

Father, thank you for your amazing creation of our bodies. Be with me and help me to talk to my kids about sex at the appropriate times and in the right ways. I want my kids to know I am here for them at all times and that I am here to help them and guide them through life. I pray for open doors for our discussions and for smooth conversations. Thank you loving us and for helping me. In Jesus's name, amen.

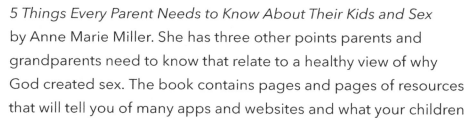

Digging Deeper

- *5 Things Every Parent Needs to Know About Their Kids and Sex* by Anne Marie Miller. She has three other points parents and grandparents need to know that relate to a healthy view of why God created sex. The book contains pages and pages of resources that will tell you of many apps and websites and what your children will see on these sites and can do on them. Miller has great wisdom. She looks at the sexual development of children and talks about how to initiate conversations about sex.

- *God's Design for Sex* books by Stan and Brenna Jones

  Book 1: *The Story of Me*, ages 3 to 5

  Book 2: *Before I Was Born*, ages 5 to 8

  Book 3: *What's the Big Deal?*, ages 8 to 11

  Book 4: *God's Design for Sex*, ages 11 to 14

- *Passport 2 Purity Getaway Kit: A life-changing getaway with your preteen*, by Dennis and Barbara Rainey, with books and CDs

"Yep, that's what happens when you share your toothbrush. I'm never sharing my toothbrush. Ever!"

MY FIVE-YEAR-OLD NIECE

(AFTER HEARING THAT WE WERE EXPECTING A BABY)

Notes

Celebrate

> *The memory of the righteous is blessed.*
> **PROVERBS 10:7 NKJV**

Every day your children are forming memories of their childhood from many different events. You might have great childhood memories that were very celebratory, like a birthday party or vacation. You might also remember simple things like playing baseball with your neighborhood friends. There are no parameters on what forms a memory, but you can help to cultivate moments that will be memorable. As I mentioned earlier, when my kids were little, I tried to plan one fun or out-of-the-ordinary event each week our family would remember as a pleasant adventure. With just a little bit of planning, you can turn a rather mundane, routine week into one that will be a great memory maker.

After we all got our chores done on Saturday mornings, we would take some time to be together outdoors, or we would have other families over for dinner and games.

We had a Fourth of July tradition of spending the holiday with the same family every year, which our kids anticipated. Another favorite family memory was of our Thanksgiving tradition of going to my husband's aunt and uncle's farm. Our kids still talk about the adventures they had on the farm. Our family even has favorite movies we like to watch on certain holidays. We look forward to it all year! For birthdays, we had little traditions that meant a lot to our kids. Kids will have memories of many things—some you can control and some you can't. For kids, the things they tend to remember most are moments in time that really stand out for some reason.

It is so important that we all have things we look forward to. Traditions help us to anticipate a moment in time with excitement, and they help unify a family through that moment. They create a family loyalty—kids of all ages rely on  tradition to help them feel stable, secure, and loved. Whether they're five, fifteen, or twenty-five, kids know there are some things the family loves to do together each year, and they look forward to them. Even better, those family traditions will draw your kids home and create a desire to be there for it every year. Your kids won't want to miss out on the tradition!

Traditions and memories don't have to be a result of grand events or holidays. Even something like having pizza every Friday night or having a pool party on the last day of school each year becomes a lasting, positive memory for kids. Ordinary events can be super fun and memorable for your kids. You can also make memories by working together on a project.

When our kids were in middle school, they really wanted a trampoline. We were beginning to work with our kids on earning money, saving, and making wise purchases. We had a proposition for our kids to "earn" their trampoline. At the time, Mike was overseeing the building of the house we would live in for years. We offered to pay our kids to be the cleanup crew to earn the money for their trampoline. They jumped at the opportunity! We wanted our trampoline to be in-ground, so the kids also began digging the hole. We soon discovered this job was too big, so to speak, for two middle schoolers, and we rented a Bobcat to expedite the process. Haha! But our kids learned a lesson in working together and earning money for something they really wanted. They still tell stories about when they "dug" the trampoline hole. It was a great memory.

When Mike was the missions director at the church we were on staff at, Sarah and Shaun were in elementary school. At Christmas we would drive down to Mexico and take other families and youth with us to hand out food and clothing. We did that at one of the dumps there and at several churches. It was very impacting to me, and I know it was to them too, to see people going through the trash to find food and seeing houses made out of cardboard. When we got back and were in our warm house with plenty of food and clothing, I realized how blessed we were and how people in other countries don't live like we do in America.

Because of Mike's position at church, we had opportunities to have the missionaries who came to speak at the church stay with us or come over for dinner and spend extended times of sharing. We heard their stories of how they were sharing the love of Jesus with people in different countries and some of the hardships they went through to do that.

Mike and I made five trips into China smuggling in Bibles in the '80s and '90s, and recently, our own church has built five churches in Thailand. During his high school years, Shaun went to Panama, Nepal, and South Africa. Sarah went to El Salvador, and I believe it was because of those first mission trips we took, and the memories from them together as a family, that God put a love in the children's hearts for people of all nations. I have always said we are either goers or senders because God would have no one perish and be lost (2 Peter 3:9).

Make sure to take lots of pictures of your children in everyday settings. You can go back later and talk about those moments and help them remember the events or occasions. Kids love looking at pictures of themselves, and you can bring in Scriptural truths and help build their self-esteem by pointing out something they did that was noble or a character trait they were displaying when the picture was taken. Taking pictures is so easy these days because of our phones!

So many simple day-to-day things can be made into wonderful memories for them with just a little planning and conversation, memories they'll have for a very long time!

> The most beautiful things are not associated with money; they are memories and moments. If you don't celebrate those, they can pass you by.
> **ALEK WEK**

> The one thing I need to leave behind is good memories.
> **MICHAEL LANDON**

When I graduate from earth to heaven, I know that although I will no longer be on earth with my family and friends, I will continue to live on in their lives through all the good memories. And those memories last for all eternity.

Take a Step

At dinner one night, talk with your family about their favorite traditions or things you do as a family. Make sure to take note of what each person says. Each person will probably have different memories and suggestions. If you don't have a lot of family traditions, there is no time like the present! Start today or at the next holiday. Keep a list in your phone of ideas you have for family traditions and mark it on your calendar. Also, if there is a project around the house that is kid appropriate, recruit your kids to help with the incentive of a movie night and pizza. Think outside the box, but also remember you don't have to force anything. Memories have more to do with living in the moment and less to do with making a huge, intricate plan.

Lean In

Father, thank you for the amazing mind you have given us to remember things. I want my kids to look back on their childhoods with happy, positive memories. I want them to enjoy being with our family and feel connected. Help me to know when and how to celebrate a moment. Your love is so strong and deep, and I want my family to be filled with it. I want to celebrate life because of what you have done for us. In Jesus's name, amen.

11am: Grill hot dogs and fries
12pm: Jump on the trampoline
2pm: Make snow cones
3pm: Watch cartoons
6pm: Dance party
Parent: "Okay, kids, time for your bath."
Kids: "You're no fun!"

Notes

Got Sleep?

> *I will both lie down in peace, and sleep;*
> *for You alone, O Lord, make me dwell in safety.*
> **PSALM 4:8 NKJV**

This is always a big question from parents: "Should I let my child sleep with me?" My answer is always a resounding *no!* Of course, there will be times for cuddling and playing in the parents' bed before they go to their own beds or at times in the morning after everyone is awake or when a child isn't feeling well. But on a regular basis, you are much better off if you don't.

Janice G. Tracht, MSW, says,

> So how does the parental bed become a "hotbed" of trouble when children are allowed to sleep through the night with their parents? Privacy and the very important things it provides for a couple are sacrificed. One of those important "things" privacy provides for is sex. Yeah . . . sex, that rather essential feature of a rich and full marriage. What happens to that fundamental means of sharing emotional closeness in a marriage when the child's demands for comfort in the marital bed supersede the need for the parents' privacy?[1]

---

1   Janice G. Tracht, MSW, "Should Children Sleep with their Parents?" Associated Counselors & Therapists, accessed June 12, 2019, http://www.beachpsych.com/pages/cc101.html.

There are healthy boundaries formed when a child knows that Mom and Dad have their bedroom and a child is separate from that.

There is a separation between the generations that functions to maintain a balance of power and appropriate intimacy. These boundaries do not exist to restrict the flow of love between members, but rather allow parents to share and benefit from mature adult intimacy, while fostering a loving and nurturing flow of parental affection to the children. When these boundaries are blurred or crossed, the marital relationship suffers.[2]

Janice continues to point out that at times, if there is difficulty in a marriage and couples aren't meeting each other's needs, they tend to try to have their children meet their emotional needs (which no child is able to do) by allowing them to sleep with them.

When our children would wake up at night scared or not feeling well and come into our room, one of us would usually walk them back to their room and stay with them for a while to bring comfort. We would pray and talk with them and tell them we would either come back and check on them or stay until they were asleep.

Children move around a lot at night and can disrupt a parent's sleep pretty consistently if they are allowed to sleep with the parents. We all know from experience that we function much better if we have a good night's sleep. So go ahead and set some boundaries for your children when they sleep, and everyone will live more happily ever after.

RESTED Parents = HAPPY Family

---

2   Tracht, "Should Children Sleep with their Parents?"

Take a Step

Identify what sleep needs the members of your family have. Are you all getting that amount of sleep? Why or why not? Are there identifiable causes for lack of sleep? Does one of your children need to be sleep trained? Or have you allowed unhealthy behavior to grow into habits? Take control, and make a plan for things you can control like bedtime and bedtime distractions. Maybe your child needs a more consistent bedtime routine that includes a story or song. Or maybe your one-year-old is still waking up through the night to eat, and they just need to be trained to stay sleeping through the night. Most cities have many sleep experts or coaches these days. You can also talk to your pediatrician about helpful ways to move into a better sleep system. You can also find great advice, articles, and help online. Don't go another night with bad sleep!

Lean In

Father, I thank you for your promise to give your beloved sweet sleep. Help us to get to the root of the sleep issues in our home and to resolve them quickly and smoothly. I declare that our home is a place of total peace and that bedtime becomes a happy, healthy, relaxed time. Show me what I need to modify or change to cultivate an atmosphere conducive to awesome sleep for our whole family. I rest in your love and joy, and I know you are with me in this season. I love you, Lord. In Jesus's name, amen.

Digging Deeper

- Janice G. Tracht, MSW, "Should Children Sleep with their Parents?" at http://www.beachpsych.com/pages/cc101.html.

> *"People who say they sleep like a baby usually don't have one."*
>
> **LEO J. BURKE**

Notes

Communication

> *Let no corrupt communication proceed out of your mouth, but that which is good to the use of edifying, that it may minister grace unto the hearers.*
> **EPHESIANS 4:29 KJV**

It was important to me to include a few chapters in this book on marriage. For those of you who are married, your marriage is the nucleus of the home, and that relationship affects the rest of the family. For those of you who are not married, you can benefit from these chapters as well, as marriage could be right around the corner for you.

Your children will grow up and likely get married. The more information and knowledge we have about marriage, the more we can help our kids navigate those relationships in the future. As I have written before, Mike and I both came from stable homes where both parents were present and involved in our upbringing. However, after our marriage and honeymoon, we soon discovered there were many days when we would reach an impasse in our communication. We became stuck in how to express our needs or expectations of each other.

I would usually get mad at Mike for some reason and use the silent treatment because I thought he should have known what I needed or expected in any given situation. Sometimes he would get frustrated or angry at me and raise his voice to communicate his displeasure, and it would cause me to retreat and feel intimidated about sharing my feelings.

We attended a Marriage Encounter weekend about ten years into our marriage. We learned some very good tools that helped us to communicate more effectively. One was called dialoging. It works like this:

- Several times a week, the husband and wife set aside fifteen to thirty minutes to write down their feelings to a particular question either the husband or the wife wants to discuss.
- It involves writing down your feelings about a particular thing that happened, or a future event, or any situation that has arisen.

DIALOGING STEPS ←

- An example could be, "How did it make you feel when we saw we had a bounced check?" or "How did it make you feel when I forgot your birthday?" or "How did it make you feel when I was late?"
- Each person writes for fifteen minutes, then lets the other person read through twice what the other person wrote. Then they talk about what each other was feeling with the intent to gain a better understanding of their mate.

After reading *Communication: Key to Your Marriage* by H. Norman Wright, we also learned the importance of learning how to send "I" messages instead of "you" messages when communicating with our spouse, children, or coworkers. An example of that would be "I was really hurt and disappointed when you interrupted me so much tonight at the party." The person's feelings were shared without putting the other person on the defensive. An example of a "you" message would be "You make me so mad because you constantly interrupt me when I am talking, and we have talked about you doing this before." The "you" message, while it can be accurate, puts the other person on the defensive and can shut down any other communication on the subject. This is because the other person will be more intent on defending themselves rather than trying to understand how the spouse is feeling.

Active listening is also a very important tool when communicating. When you are actively listening to people, you are giving them your full attention, and you are able to say back to them, "What I hear you saying is that you did not think I was telling the truth when I said _____." Before you, as a listener, give any response, you make sure you have heard the person accurately and understand them.

I wish I could say that after forty-seven years of marriage we have mastered the use of all these tools in communication on a regular basis. We have not, but we still work to put these into practice when we have disagreements. Sometimes we just react instead of responding with skill in our communicating.

Not too long ago we did a teaching series at our church on communication and reviewed all the things I have mentioned. We don't always know how much other people were helped, but it helped us to remember once again the Scripture that says, "Let your [communication] be gracious and effective so that you will have the right answer for everyone" (Colossians 4:6 NLT). I would add "especially for your mate."

What has also been helpful to me to learn about communication is the ability to request from Mike what I need. To be able to say, "I want to share some things with you, but I just need you to listen and not try to fix it or look for a solution" is great. The funny thing is that now we have reversed roles in some areas and ways of thinking, and it is him I hear telling me frequently, "I just need you to listen to me right now, not give me a solution or try to fix it." I tend to think I have to fix everything. As I am learning to communicate with him the thing I need, or he is stating what he needs, it simplifies our communication.

I am a hard worker, but I also need one fun thing to look forward to doing each week. It is part of my Sanguine temperament. Over the years we have gotten into the routine of me planning something fun for us to do together every Friday, which is our day off. It has become our date day! We have to guard our time, because if we aren't careful, we can end up working or letting other things crowd out our time together. Most Fridays we don't have all day together, but at least part of the day is dedicated to being together and going beyond surface communication.

When we recently taught on communication tools on a Sunday morning, we encouraged the congregation to teach these concepts to their children also. They will have a real advantage in life, in business, and in the home if they can understand and operate in these principles at an early age. One member of our congregation is a preschool teacher, and she said she started teaching about "you and I" messages that next week.

Take a Step

Start practicing "you and I" communicating. Approach conversations with your spouse from the perspective of understanding or wanting to see eye to eye instead of only noticing the differences. Let yourself see your spouse through a filter of love and grace rather than of bitterness and misunderstanding.

Start to be clear about your needs and desires, and ask your husband about his needs and desires. Let the conversations in your home be judgment-free zones for the whole family. When people feel free to communicate their feelings, they won't feel like they need to keep secrets or hide things.

Lean In

Father, thank you for watching over my mouth and teaching me what to say. I know you care about the dynamics of my marriage and the atmosphere in my home. Help us to be loving participants in healthy, open communication. Lead and guide us into all truth by your Holy Spirit, and help us experience the fullness of a loving, honest, fulfilling relationship—as you've created it to be. In Jesus's name, amen.

Digging Deeper

There are scores of books out there on marriage and communication, but still some of my favorites are:

- *Communication: Key to Your Marriage* by H. Norman Wright
- *The Act of Marriage: The Beauty of Sexual Love* by Tim and Beverly LaHaye
- *Love Works: Develop Healthy Relationships in a "Love Broken" World* by Philip and Holly Wagner

"Marriage is like a walk in the park, Jurassic Park."

Notes

More Notes

Discipline Is Love

> *When we are punished, it seems to us at the time something to make us sad, not glad. Later, however, those who have been disciplined by such punishment reap the peaceful reward of a righteous life.*
>
> **HEBREWS 12:11 GNT**

One of the first Scriptures our children learned was Ephesians 6:1-3 (NKJV): "Children, obey your parents in the Lord, for this is right. 'Honor your father and mother,' which is the first commandment with promise: that it may be well with you, and you may live long on the earth."

God says in this verse there is a twofold promise for children who obey this word. The first one is that all will go well with our children. What does that mean?

When things go well, your children will have an intimate relationship with Jesus Christ. They will be able to choose godly friends. They will be able to succeed and do well in school and later in college or specialized training; they will choose the right mate and will be committed and trustworthy. It means your children will be able to obtain and maintain a good job and will be able to pay their bills. If it is well with them, they will have a good, open relationship with you. They will want to spend time around you; they will look forward to holidays because of the special memories you've created through the years. They will want their spouse and your grandchildren to experience what they relish. God wants it to be well with them in every relationship and aspect of life.[1]

I would like to add to this list that God wants them "to be in health and prosper just as [their] soul prospers" (3 John 2 NASB), and that His favor would surround them like a shield (Psalm 5:12). He also says "There shall be no evil befall you, nor any plague or calamity will come near your tent" (Psalm 91:10 AMPC).

Ephesians 6 says our children will live long on the earth when they obey us as parents (v. 1–3). We all want our children living long on the earth.

God PROMISES Long Life FOR OBEDIENCE

The definition of *discipline* is training that is expected to produce a specific character trait or pattern of behavior, especially training that produces moral or mental improvement. Training is to fix incorrect behavior or create better skills. Many forms of discipline and training are available to use to help our kids in their growth.

- It is very important to use praise and rewards with your kids when they are making correct choices. This is motivating and encouraging to them as well to other siblings.

- Also give plenty of time for transitions from one activity or event to another. For example, saying, "Five more minutes until we need to leave," helps your children mentally disconnect from the current activity to the next one slowly, and doing so can reduce their frustration of having to stop what they're doing.

- Another form of instilling self-control and self-discipline into their lives is to use time-out for small things that come up

---

1   David and Roxanne Swann, *Guarantee Your Child's Success* (Tulsa: Harrison House, 1990), 11.

during the day, like your children not wanting to share or give a sibling a turn at something they are doing. About one minute in time-out for each year they are old is the usual guideline. They can go and think about it and come back with a better attitude, or be willing to share after having a time of exclusion from the activity everyone else is doing.

- Another way to help develop self-discipline is to delay self-gratification for a few minutes or so, depending on their age. I remember one time Sarah was playing in the play area and was ready to come out, but I couldn't come help her get out, and I said, "You are going to have to wait a few minutes until Mommy can come get you." She did, and I think she was about six or seven months old at the time.

- As they get older, another example of self-discipline is helping them save money from their allowance for a big item and not spend it all the minute they get it.

- It is also so important to know if your child is hungry and tired. I call that being hangry. When your children are in that place and in meltdown mode, the most important thing you can do is feed them and get them down for a nap. Their ability to reason or comply is very low at this point.

- Another few tips I have used with my children is to give them things they can be in charge of or have control over. They love to help and have a sense of accomplishment when they finish things.

- Taking away privileges is another form of discipline and training that helps them learn to obey you and follow the rules of the house.

- Redirecting their focus from one thing to another is also a way of discipline that helps them to make a choice from what they want to do to what you see them needing to do. For example:

"It is too cold to go outside, so let's see if we can make a tent under the table."

Consistency is key is all these areas of discipline and training. Disciplining children is as much about you yourself being a disciplined, consistent parent.

There is a proper use of the rod as another form of discipline that at times needs to be applied to our children. Our job as parents is to know and understand how to instill character and self-discipline into our children so they will obey us. God shows us how to do that in His Word. It is not necessarily easy, but there are several ways we can do this. I'll define some terms that many times get intertwined together.

The proper use of the "rod of correction" is referred to in Proverbs 13:24; 22:15; 23:13-14; 29:15. This is commonly referred to as a spanking. There will be times in your child's life when it will be necessary to use this form of correction, like when you see deliberate disobedience and rebellion to established rules and codes of conduct—rules that have been set up and explained clearly to your child. For example, things like lying, refusing to obey, throwing tantrums, spitting or biting someone, doing anything that would hurt themselves or another person would warrant the proper use of the rod. I will go over those steps in a little bit.

I had to remind myself that children are born with a selfish (sinful) nature. (Jeremiah 17:9 says our hearts are deceitful above all things and exceedingly corrupt. That is why we need to be born again.) Children will challenge their parents' authority because they very simply want their own way. One of the seasons of parenting where this begins is at around two years of age. We have to remember we are exerting external control *on* them and in the process, self-control is being developed *in* them. This is what God has laid out for us to do. We have to trust Him that as we do this in faith, just like the Word says, it will produce a peaceable reward in our children.

Their self-discipline is the reward from our external discipline. I hope that makes sense. We really need to understand this, or we just won't do it. Today we see that we are in a culture totally against doing this. Correction has been grossly misused, but it was never God's plan to abuse our children, nor will it ever be. The proper use of the rod of

RULES OF HOUSE MUST BE CLEAR

correction is not hitting your child with your hand or slamming them up against the wall. God would never sanction that.

It is important that the rules of the house, so to speak, are clear, and that your children understand what will happen if those rules are not followed, and that both parents are in agreement with carrying out the event. And it should be an event.

Proper use of the rod communicates love. "He who spares his rod hates his son, but he who loves him disciplines him diligently" (Proverbs 13:24 NKJV). *The Message* translation says, "A refusal to correct is a refusal to love; love your children by disciplining them." Another reason for disciplining your child is because it prevents the parents from being shamed. Proverbs 29:15 says, "The rod and reproof give wisdom, but a child who gets his own way brings shame to his mother." Children thrive when they know the boundaries, and house rules are very helpful in knowing what boundaries of behavior they are to have.

Understanding one very important concept helped me to go beyond my mercy motivation and move into obedience to do what God said to do concerning the proper use of the rod and discipline. Revelation came to me with this statement,

Every child is born with a selfish (sinful) nature and will challenge parental authority as they get older. Through discipline a child learns to yield to loving parental authority, and in turn can learn that this yielding is good to other authorities as well. Discipline produces pain that is for your child's good. Each child is unique and is motivated towards good behavior differently. Spanking should be used wisely in the process of training your child. Spanking has several benefits; it re-establishes who is in charge, it restores the relationship and can be use for reproof and correction.[2]

It is critical your child knows what the rules are before you begin to use the rod correctly. Don't provide too many little rules; just stick  with a few big age-appropriate rules your kids can remember and fulfill. Preschoolers are old enough to know they shouldn't hit or hurt a sibling. They also can learn to be quick to obey. Again, spanking is not appropriate for every time your kid messes up. Give them time to learn and practice the rules.

Mike and I decided that when we needed to spank our children for disobedience or rebellion, it would be an event and we would have specific guidelines we would follow:

1. The first thing after a known rule was broken was to send Sarah or Shaun to the bedroom and prepare for a spanking.
2. We retrieved the rod from the top of the refrigerator or from my purse if we were at someone else's house. I think one very important thing that happens when you use a rod (like a paint stick or wooden spoon) and not your hand (hands are for loving) is that it gives you time to cool down and not spank out of your anger but when you are in control of your emotions.
3. We would briefly explain why they were getting the rod.
4. We asked them to lie over their bed.

---

2   *Principles for Effective Parenting*, FamilyLife, out of print.

5. We would give two or three swats. It would and should sting. They should cry.

6. After they stopped crying, we would ask them what Ephesians 6:1 said. They would repeat the verse, and we would say, "Do you want things to go well with you?" They would say yes. "Do you want to live a long time?" They would say yes. We would explain that just like they had to obey us, we had to obey God and use the rod when they disobeyed. (We had gone over the many Scriptures with them about the proper use of the rod.)

7. Then we would have them pray and ask God to forgive them and ask us to forgive them for being disobedient. We would say that we loved them and wait until they said they loved us. We kissed and hugged, and then off they went. Mike's idea was to have them tell us that they loved us to help them learn at an early age that love was a decision and not based on an emotion.

We felt like spankings should be done in private and as quickly as possible. Some parents would ask us if they should pull the child's pants down and then spank the child. We never agreed with that idea. It felt more like humiliation than correction and training.

Mike and I did not spank over accidents, but when an accident occurred, they did need to help clean up the mess or help pay for something that was broken if they were old enough. We didn't spank for every little thing, but only when a rule had been deliberately broken.

DISCIPLINE
→ NOT ←
HUMILIATE

Each child will be disciplined differently. Sarah didn't receive as many spankings as Shaun did, and she would respond and remember faster than Shaun did. Shaun would act and then think about his actions, whereas Sarah was more cautious and thought through things more before she acted.

I remember a situation with Sarah after she had received a spanking. Mike told her he loved her, but she wouldn't tell him she loved him, so Mike just said that he would wait until she decided to say it because he knew she loved him. After a while she did say it—when she had moved beyond her emotions in the moment from her head to a decision she had in her heart.

As both Sarah and Shaun got to upper elementary school, a few times we used the rod for correction for a bad attitude rather than an action. You know what I am talking about—the huffing and puffing around and the rolling of the eyes when asked to do something they didn't want to do. Those are symptoms of rebellion in attitude rather than an action.

Mike and I get asked a lot about the use of time-out. I think time-out is effective on some personalities more than others. A child that likes to be alone will not see time-out as part of correction and discipline. We used time-out when one of our kids wasn't willing to share or said something that wasn't polite or mannerly. They would go to their room to think about their actions and come back after so many minutes to talk about the right course of action. This is an appropriate consequence for smaller misbehaviors.

When I was a child, I got many more spankings than my younger brother. I think he learned from me on what not to do. I know my mom gave me some spankings; however, what stands out in my mind is what I got a spanking for over and over again. There was a playground very close to our house where we lived. I was in elementary school, and most of the neighborhood kids spent a lot of summer evenings playing there. The rule at my house was that I had to be home before dark or as it was getting dark. Time after time I would be totally lost in playing, and someone would say, "Sheri, here comes your dad." I would look up and there he would be, walking toward the playground with belt in hand.

After doing some research on the rod, I realized the reason a rod is chosen to bring correction is that it can be used on the spot on the body with the largest amount of padding. When you use a belt, the belt falls over on the side of the child's leg and can cause a welt due to the lack of fat located there. I would usually start trying to talk my dad out of a spanking all the way home. I was quite remorseful and explained over and over again how I just lost track of time, but to no avail.

One night in particular when I saw him coming, I thought up an ingenious plan to run home ahead of him by taking a shortcut through one of the neighbors' yards. So off I ran like the wind, and when I got home, I noticed the bathroom door was closed. I opened it, and my mom was in the bathtub. Quick as lightning I peeled off my clothes and got right in the tub with her. I never said a word as to why. A few minutes later, my dad came back home and opened the bathroom door. He saw his angelic daughter in the bathtub and burst out laughing. Whew . . . saved by the tub.

I've placed many Scriptures concerning the proper use of the rod at the end of this chapter. I really encourage you to pray about them and see that the One who created us knows what is best for us. The proper use of the rod takes great discipline and consistency on our part to be effective.

One of the greatest challenges for me as a parent was to be consistent in using the rod properly. There were so many days when I yelled rather than just simply did what I knew I should do. I always said that to have a disciplined child, you have to be disciplined yourself. Thank heavens the Lord helped me to be consistent, but even more than that, His grace helped make up for when we failed and fell short as parents. We don't have to think it is all in our ability to raise and train our children, but rather that His grace and wisdom will provide all we are lacking. "No discipline brings joy, but seems sad and painful; yet to those who have been trained by it, afterwards it yields the peaceful fruit of righteousness [right standing with God and a lifestyle and attitude that seeks conformity to God's will and purpose]" (Hebrews 12:11 AMP).

Other forms of correction are about disciplining and training with our words by talking to our children about choices they have made and why or why not they were wise or not beneficial at the time. We call those teachable moments. As your children get older, these opportunities are very valuable for them so they can learn by their mistakes.

Take a Step

Sit down with your spouse and clearly outline parameters for discipline in your home. Be very specific about the behaviors that warrant a spanking. Your list should be small—too many rules create a dictatorship system that is begging to be rebelled against. Keep your rules simple: obey God, parents, and authority; no lying; and so on. To be clear, every childhood behavior does *not* need to be punished by spanking. You must be very understanding about what is a teachable moment and what is a rebellious action that deserves discipline. After you have outlined the discipline parameters in your home, discuss them with your children and go over the Scriptures about the use of the rod with them so they know why you need to use the rod and what God has said about it. Use praise and rewards very generously too.

Lean In

Father, more than anything, I want my children to live the purpose-filled, happy, peaceful life you have intended for them. I need your help to do this. Lead me so I can be consistent. I declare that my children are obedient and will live in great peace, for they are taught of you, Lord. My kids will live long lives on the earth. We are training up our children in the way they should go, and they will not depart from it. Help us to distinguish between rebellion and innocent mistakes. Also, help us to nurture and shape our kids for who they are so we are not shaping them to be someone other than the unique individuals you created them to be. Thank you so much for your love and guidance. In Jesus's name, amen.

Digging Deeper

· *Guarantee Your Child's Success* by David and Roxanne Swann
· *Principles for Effective Parenting* by Family Life.

> "When your mom voice is so loud, even your neighbors brush their teeth and get dressed."

BONUS! → Verses on Discipline

"Those who withhold the rod hate their children, but the one who loves them applies discipline." (Proverbs 13:24 CEB)

"Discipline and teach your son while there is hope, and do not [indulge your anger or resentment by imposing inappropriate punishment nor] desire his destruction." (Proverbs 19:18 AMP)

"Foolishness is bound up in the heart of a child; the rod of discipline [correction administered with godly wisdom and lovingkindness] will remove it far from him." (Proverbs 22:15 AMP)

"Do not hold back discipline from the child; if you swat him with a reed-like rod [applied with godly wisdom] he will not die." (Proverbs 23:13 AMP)

"The rod and reproof (godly instruction) give wisdom, but a child who gets his own way brings shame to his mother." (Proverbs 29:15 AMP)

"Correct your son, and he will give you comfort; yes, he will delight your soul." (Proverbs 29:17 AMP)

"My son, do not reject or take lightly the discipline of the Lord, [learn from your mistakes and the testing that comes from His correction through discipline]; nor despise His rebuke, for those whom the Lord loves He corrects, even as a father corrects the son in whom he delights." (Proverbs 3:11–12 AMP)

"Do what your father tells you and never forget what your mother taught you. Keep their words with you always, locked in your heart. . . . Their instructions are a shining light; their correction can teach you how to live." (Proverbs 6:20–21, 23 GNT)

"To accept correction is wise, to reject it is stupid." (Proverbs 12:1 CEV)

"A wise son pays attention when his father corrects him, but an arrogant person never admits he is wrong." (Proverbs 13:1 GNB)

"Poverty and shame will come to him who neglects discipline, but he who regards reproof will be honored." (Proverbs 13:18 NASB)

"Refuse discipline and end up homeless; embrace correction and live an honored life." (Proverbs 13:18 MSG)

"A fool doesn't like a father's instruction, but those who heed correction are mature." (Proverbs 15:5 CEB)

"An undisciplined, self-willed life is puny; an obedient, God willed life is spacious." (Proverbs 15:32 MSG)

"Listen to counsel and accept discipline, that you may be wise the rest of your days." (Proverbs 19:20 NASB)

"Cease listening, my son, to instruction and discipline and you will stray from the words of knowledge." (Proverbs 19:27 AMP).

"For the time being no discipline brings joy, but seems sad and painful; yet to those who have been trained by it, afterwards it yields the peaceful fruit of righteousness [right standing with God and a lifestyle and attitude that seeks conformity to God's will and purpose]." (Hebrews 12:11 AMP).

Usually, one parent tends to be bent more toward the law side of things and the other parent more lenient or grace-oriented. It is very important for parents to become a little of both and not one or the other. It is not fair for one parent to always be the one to discipline your children and the other not to. No matter what our personalities are, both parents should operate on these scriptures and principles and there should be a balance.

More Notes

Seasons in Parenting

*There is a time for everything
and a season to every activity under heaven.*

ECCLESIASTES 3:1 NIV

One very certain thing about life is that we have four different seasons a year. We know what to anticipate in each season. We know what to wear and how to plan activities according to the season we are in. Knowing these things in advance helps us to know what to do in each season—we know each season will be marked by different events and milestones. Many of the ideas in this chapter stem from John Rosemond's fantastic book on this approach, *Parenting by the Book*.

> Like farming, raising livestock, gathering maple syrup, and the migrations of fish and birds, the raising of children is marked by seasons. These seasons were established by God; therefore, they cannot be altered at the whim of man. . . . Parents who conform their behavior to the unique requirements of each of the seasons of child rearing will be all but assured a "high yield" of reward and satisfaction out of seeing their children advance toward and eventually claim responsible maturity.[1]
>
> **JOHN ROSEMOND,** *PARENTING BY THE BOOK*

---

1   John Rosemond, *Parenting by The Book: Biblical Wisdom for Raising Your Child* (New York: Simon and Schuster, 2013) 169-170.

I like to think of the first season as the Season of Serving. We have a new baby born into the world, and he or she is totally dependent on the mother and father. Children can do absolutely nothing for themselves. They will eat, sleep, cry, and fill many diapers. Rosemond says this stage lasts approximately two years. There is a near-constant ministry of surveillance and "doing"—checking, feeding, carrying, changing, comforting, fixing, fetching, and so on.

The purposes of season one are three fold:

1. To "root" the child securely in the world—to assure him he is where he belongs, with people who love him and who will take good and proper care of him under any and all circumstances.

2. To provide for the child's fundamental biological needs—put bluntly, to keep him alive and thriving.

3. To prevent, as much as is humanly possible, the child from hurting himself.[2]

When Shaun was about six months old and was in his swing one day, I kept seeing Sarah walk in from the backyard to the swing. She was extra quiet. I walked over to where she was standing and saw she had been putting rocks from the yard neatly into her brother's mouth. Without totally freaking out, I began to tell her in the calmest voice I could muster that rocks are one thing we *don't* put in her brother's mouth!

A few years ago, I was laughing about this very thing with our son-in-law, Jason. Sarah and Jason's son, Bryce, was seventeen months old and had started walking. He was into everything and wanted to know how everything works. He would put almost everything in his mouth

---

2   Rosemond, 170.

and opened and closed cabinets and doors with great passion. He was just able to indicate to us when he was unhappy about something or didn't get what he wanted by shaking his head and crying. He also could let us know when he did want something by pointing to it or taking our finger and leading us to the room, toy, or food he wanted.

The next season in parenting begins around or a little before age 2 and has a lot to do with discipline. We will call this the Season of Leadership and Authority. During this season it is the parent's job to govern the child in such a way that he (1) consents to their government (becomes a willing disciple), and (2) internalizes their discipline and gradually develops the self-restraint necessary to govern himself responsibly."[3]

I've devoted a very long chapter to the proper use of the rod and the Scriptures that explain why using it is so important, as well as other methods of discipline, and I've also emphasized making sure all your children understand they are loved unconditionally.

SEASON OF LEADERSHIP & AUTHORITY

Our children both received the proper use of the rod, but Shaun, like myself, had the visitation more often. This stage of frequent course correction lasts until around third or fourth grade. This season is also when your kids will learn to dress themselves and to do some of their own personal hygiene like brushing their teeth and washing their hands. They will begin to learn that they can't hit or hurt their siblings and that they can pick up their toys and help with simple tasks. This season lasts from about three to thirteen.

The next stage is the Season of Mentoring. In this season the child

---

3   Rosemond, 173.

has completed the disciplinary "curriculum" of season two and is now regarded as mostly self-governing. He or she no longer needs adults to tell him what to do and what not to do; rather, he needs adult mentors to help him acquire the practical skills he will need to emancipate successfully—how to apply for a job, balance a budget, plan for the future, and the like.[4]

Shaun had been on several mission trips throughout his high school years, and after his senior year, he wasn't really interested in going right into college. Our church had been involved in Teen Mania ministry, and they were hosting an information weekend for parents and their kids to get acquainted with the ministry. To make a long story short, he really loved the ministry and wanted to do a year's internship there. The first young men we met there were Chris Hart and Chano Trevino. The three of them did the internship, and to this day they are still best friends and are raising their own children together! God has got a plan for your child!

Sarah also went on a mission trip in high school, and our contact with several missionary families was very impacting for all of us during that season. We are still friends with them to this day.

This is also an important age at which to begin to let the rope out a little, so to speak. Give your kids a bit more freedom as they prove themselves trustworthy. I believe it was Shaun's junior or senior year in high school when he wanted to go to several graduation or end-of-year parties in one night. I didn't feel really good about him trying to make the rounds to so many parties, and I told him so, but we let him go. We got a call about eleven or so that night, and he had run out of gas. When he went to fill the gas can, someone broke out his front

---

4   Rosemond, 173, 174.

window and stole his battery. He, of course, felt bad, and we knew the Holy Spirit had been trying to warn him and us, but we just overrode the feeling. I have seen that when parents don't let their high school kids have a little independence, they very often don't know how to handle the freedom when they are in college, and they can make some poor choices and decisions they regret later. As we let our kids have a little more independence and watch as mistakes are made, we can be there to help them walk through them.

The next season in parenting is the college years and after and is called the "friendship season."[5] This is where your children, under direction and guidance, can successfully live by themselves and pursue their God-given purposes in life. They might ask you for advice sometimes, but more and more they are growing with God to be independent.

And, of course, being the parent of an adult child is the last season. You do a lot of listening in this season, and you make suggestions and give advice when they ask for it. Remind them at times of things they already know but maybe haven't been doing. It's important to schedule time with them to do things together and to ask them for advice occasionally. It really becomes more like a relationship you have with good friends. Hopefully there will be times of laughing and having fun together and letting them make mistakes without you saying, "I told you so."

Shaun attended Oral Roberts University (ORU) in Tulsa, Oklahoma, and Sarah went to ORU for a year but ended up coming back to Albuquerque and graduating from the University of New Mexico.

Our kids followed the paths they felt they were supposed to travel on. Each one had a slightly different path, but through prayer

---

5   Rosemond, 174.

and God's guidance, they walked it out successfully. Today they are both involved in ministry with their spouses and are raising happy grandchildren for Mike and me to enjoy.

We had ups and downs as they were growing up. We weren't perfect parents, and they weren't perfect kids. But we aren't called to be perfect, just forgiven and walking in His grace.

There are many books that will give you exact developmental characteristics of children and what they should be doing at each age and phase of life. I have been pretty general in this chapter. However, I have given you resources and books in other chapters that will help you with knowing these things in greater detail.

Over the last twenty years, we have observed parents sometimes get messed up by getting the seasons out of order. I see parents of ten-year-olds, or five-year-olds for that matter, trying to be friends with their kids instead of being the parents. Make sure you remember you are the boss and that your kids are not always going to like your decisions. The friendship stage is the *last* season in parenting. Some of the seasons in parenting will be easier than others, but if we follow His directions, we can enjoy our children every day.

As your children move from one season to another, remember to give them a little more independence. As they demonstrate the fulfillment of their responsibilities and good judgment, they can be trusted more and more.

Take a Step

What season are you in with your kids? Are your kids in the same season or different seasons? It is vital to recognize the season each of your children is in right now and treat them appropriately for that season.

Lean In

Father, thank you for seasons of growth. Thank you for knowing we need change and variety in life. Help me to navigate the seasons of my kids' lives. Show me how to parent and train and love them appropriately. In Jesus's name, amen.

Digging Deeper

· *Parenting by the Book* by John Rosemond

> *"We spend the first twelve months of our children's lives teaching them to walk and talk and the next twelve telling them to sit down and be quiet."*

Notes

More Notes

DAY TWENTY-EIGHT

Your Kids Are Like Sponges

> *As [a man] thinks in his heart, so is he.*
> **PROVERBS 23:7 NKJV**

Children learn more quickly in their early years than at any other time in life. They need love and nurturing to develop a sense of trust and security that turns into confidence as they grow. . . .

The first five years are particularly important for the development of the child's brain, and the first three years are the most critical in shaping the child's brain architecture. Early experiences provide the base for the brain's organizational development and functioning throughout life. They have a direct impact on how children develop learning skills as well as social and emotional abilities. . . .

Child development refers to the changes that occur as a child grows and develops in relation to being physically healthy, mentally alert, emotionally sound, socially competent and ready to learn.[1]

---

1   "Facts for Life," fourth ed., Facts for Life Global, accessed June 12, 2019, http://www.factsforlifeglobal.org/resources/factsforlife-en-full.pdf, 49.

With all that in mind, it is so very important that you understand you are your children's greatest teacher and role model. They begin to imitate everything you do, even down to the "look" you give and the intonation of your voice.

Once when I was at my daughter's house, her daughter, Bailey, who at the time was playing with her nine-month-old little brother, Bryce, used a voice tone that sounded just like Sarah's and mine did when we played with Bryce. We both looked at each other and laughed. Bailey will use the same words Sarah uses, like "actually," and when frustrated, will raise her voice like her mother.

As parents, it doesn't cut it to say, "Do as I say, not as I do," because your children will imitate your behavior, mannerisms, and attitudes. That really puts a lot of pressure on us as parents to be the best example we can be. That doesn't mean we have to be perfect! I've addressed this in Day 1. It's like being quick to say you are sorry. I believe being the best parents we can be means being able to daily draw strength from the relationship we have with the Lord Jesus Christ and His Word.

Every day I knew I had to spend time with Him in order to (try to) be loving, patient, kind, and selfless. Early on, I had to come back to the fact that I was sowing great seeds of love and wisdom into my children that I would see fruit from, later in their lives . . . or I wasn't.

So much of parenting is about molding and teaching in the beginning to see the *end* result of the desired character development, "declaring the end and the result from the beginning" (Isaiah 46:10 AMP).

Mike and I talked about the things we wanted instilled in our children, and we started helping them develop in those areas early on in their preschool and elementary years. I will share with you a list of the things we wanted to instill into their lives, but ultimately you will have to pray and decide what God wants you to focus on to help your children develop godly character.

1. Know God

Our first priority was to teach our children to know and love God and be quick to obey Him. This would be a process taking many years. It would begin with us praying with our children and then, as they grew, teaching them to pray. It would also involve us providing age-appropriate devotionals as they advanced in their reading ability and maturity level. This shifts them into building their own relationship with the Lord and growing in that relationship and in the knowledge of the Word of God. "Study to show yourself approved unto God, a workman that needs not to be ashamed, rightly dividing the word of truth" (2 Timothy 2:15 AKJV).

2. Serve Well

The second character trait we wanted to develop in our children was a good work ethic. Matthew 20:26-27 (CEV) says, "You know foreign rulers like to order their people around. And their great leaders have full power over everyone they rule. But don't act like them. If you want to be first, you must be the slave of the rest."

3. Have a Well-Balanced Life

The third thing we wanted to teach our kids was to have a well-balanced, faith-filled home life that includes love, discipline, instruction, rewards, training, recreational activities, and church activities. In this they would also learn about planning, time-management, goals, organizing, and how to make everything fit together. Structure is the key here.

4. Manage Money Wisely $

The fourth objective would be to have them manage finances well. To do this, we had to teach them about tithing, saving, and wise spending. We started with piggy banks or envelopes designated for giving, saving, and spending. Help your children give their toys and clothes away on a regular basis as they outgrow them. If there is a good cause to give to, give them there. Help them learn and memorize Scriptures on giving. Acts 20:35 (AKJV): "Support the weak, and remember the words of the Lord Jesus, how he said, It is more blessed to give than to receive." Luke 6:38 (AJKV) says, "Give, and it will be given to you; good measure, pressed down, and shaken together, and running over, shall men give into you bosom." Another foundational Scripture on giving is in Malachi 3:10–11 (MSG) that says, "Bring your full tithe to the Temple treasury so there will be ample provisions in my Temple. Test me in this and see if I don't open up heaven itself to you and pour out blessings beyond your wildest dreams."

5. Stay Christ-Centered

The last objective or goal we had in training our children was to have a Christ-centered home as opposed to a child-centered home. I go into details on that in chapter 17, "Angry Kids."

Reading to your children, helping them learn how to use puzzles, board games, and blocks, and making sure they have creative playtime to use their imagination is vital to their early childhood development. Taking walks together and pointing out different flowers, bugs, people, the environment, and nature around you is important in their development. Love to a child is spelled T-I-M-E—your time with them.

Take a Step

Sit down with your spouse and identify the key character traits you want your kids to have. From there, map out a plan on how you will train them up in those areas. Discuss any bad habits or tendencies the two of you might have that you don't want to pass down to your kids. Discuss strategies to eliminate these behaviors in your home. This is a great time to also discuss the idea of a family vision statement. Keeping the vision plain in front of you and your kids creates unity and keeps your eye on the prize.

Lean In

Father, I love you so much. Thank you for gently correcting me in areas that need to change and in ways I can grow. Holy Spirit, thank you for leading and guiding us into all truth and for helping us to lead our kids that way as well. Because of your Word, we know the character traits you desire to see in your children. We are committed to being godly parents, and with your leading, we know our kids will lead happy, healthy, productive lives. In Jesus's name, amen.

Digging Deeper

· "Child Development and Early Learning" by factsforlifeglobal.org

"This morning, my wife told my three-year-old daughter that owls were nocturnal. My daughter responded, 'Yes, owls are not turtles.'"

Notes

Praying for Your Kids

> *Happy is the person who honors the Lord, who takes pleasure in obeying his commands. The good man's children will be powerful in the land; his descendants will be blessed. His family will be wealthy and rich, and he will be prosperous forever.*
>
> **PSALMS 112:1-3 GNT**

No one, except God of course, loves your children as much as you and your spouse. We have our children for a brief season of time and then they are on their own. Our prayers for them are vital throughout their lifetimes, and they are pivotal for them to fulfill the plan God has for their lives. James 5:16 says the effective prayer of a righteous person can accomplish much. We want to see God answer prayers for our children, and we know these prayers accomplish much for their lives. Few people will pray for them if we do not.

We also know that "we wrestle not against flesh and blood, but against principalities, against powers, against the rulers of the darkness of this world, against spiritual wickedness in high places" (Ephesians 6:12 KJV). We, and our children, have an enemy, Satan, who is daily trying to steal, kill, and destroy from us (John 10:10). It is especially critical that until our children are of the age to

INTERCEDE FOR YOUR KIDS

do spiritual warfare in prayer themselves, we must stand in the gap to intercede for them (Ezekiel 22:30).

There are so many wonderful books, articles, and websites about praying for your child. Ann Arkins and Gary Harrell suggest twelve character traits to pray for your child: kindness, humility, teachability, forgiveness, obedience, discernment, purity, responsibility, courage, servanthood, contentment, and endurance.[1]

YouthMin.org suggests praying for your children's godly wisdom, character, a spirit of excellence, humility, a desire to know God, for direction, for favor, discernment, for the right friends or spouse, and respect toward authority.[2]

The place to start, of course, in praying for your children is to pray for their salvation and that they receive Jesus Christ as their Lord and Savior. That is based on Romans 10:9-10 (KJV) that says, "If thou shalt confess with thy mouth the Lord Jesus, and shalt believe in thine heart that God hath raised him from the dead, thou shalt be saved. For with the heart man believeth unto righteousness and with the mouth confession is made unto salvation." I remember praying that Scripture with Sarah one day when we were sitting on the couch when she was about three years old.

The most important things to pray about for your children will also depend upon what they are going through at the time. There was a period of time when Shaun was having trouble in a particular subject at school in the third or fourth grade. As well as giving him extra help at home, Mike and I began to apply the Scriptures in Daniel 1 to Shaun. We also used these same Scriptures with Sarah when she was

---

1   Ann Arkins and Gary Harrell, *While They are Sleeping: 12 Character Traits to Pray for the Children You Love* (Little Rock, AR: Family Life, 2010), 7.

2   Ben Read, "10 Things to Pray for Your Children," YouthMin.org, March 19, 2012, https://youthmin.org/2012/03/10-things-to-pray-for-your-children/.

said to be mildly dyslexic with certain letters. We prayed and spoke these prayers over them.

> As for these four youths God gave them knowledge and skill in all learning and wisdom . . . and in all matters of wisdom and understanding concerning which the king asked them, he found them ten times better than all the [learned] magicians and enchanters who were in his whole realm.
>
> **DANIEL 1:17, 20 AMPC**

We also prayed they would be youths without blemish, well favored in appearance, and skillful in all wisdom, discernment, and understanding, apt in learning knowledge, and competent to stand and serve in the king's palace.

In a child's preschool years, some of the basic Scriptures to pray over them will have to do with getting along with their siblings and close friends. Below is a sample prayer focus based on Ephesians 4:32. Insert your child's name in the blanks:

> Be kind and compassionate to one another, forgiving each other, just as in Christ God forgave you." Loving gracious Father, help _____ to resolve his conflicts in ways that honor you, instead of harboring bitterness or anger in his heart. May he not shout angrily or say things but would be kind and loving. Give _____ the desire (and discipline, my addition) to forgive just as you have forgiven him in Christ.

As they get older, this is a Scripture they can learn and memorize also.

Sarah and Shaun both went to a Christian school until high school. At that time, they decided they wanted to go to a public high school. It was to be a very big change for them, and Mike and I knew they would experience peer pressure at a whole new level. We began to pray for discernment for them. Based on 1 Kings 3:9, we prayed for them to have an understanding mind and a hearing heart to judge and that they would discern between good and bad. We also prayed James 1:5 for them for wisdom.

Sarah and I also prayed together—based on the prayer of agreement in Matthew 18:19—for the Lord to bring her together with another Christian girl to be friends with. It was a pretty lonely first semester that ninth-grade year. She was shocked at the difference between a Christian school and a public school. She hung in there, and God brought her friend Marcia across her path for the second semester, and they remained close all during high school.

I prayed the same prayers for Shaun the summer before he was to go to public high school. Shaun had been friends with David Hicks in elementary school. When I found out David would be going to the same high school as Shaun, I contacted David's mom, Carole. We prayed together that David and Shaun would reconnect and become friends. They certainly did—they did sports together and remained friends during high school, like Sarah and Marcia.

If your children have one Christian friend during their school years, it makes a huge difference in them being able to stay steady in their faith and not crumble under the pressure of the world's influence. "Don't team up with those who are unbelievers. How can righteousness be a partner with wickedness? How can light live with darkness?" (2 Corinthians 6:14 NLT).

Mike and I also prayed for both of them for their future spouses early on in their lives. You can pray for their future spouses to be believers raised in a godly environment, that they will keep themselves pure for marriage, and that they will desire to put God first and foremost in their lives. I also prayed God would have the person He handpicked for each of them to marry. I have seen the answers to all these prayers come to produce much fruit in my children's lives. They are married to the most loving, caring, dedicated, loyal, faithful, God-loving mates I could have ever imagined. God did indeed handpick Jason and Meghan for Sarah and Shaun, and it has been exceedingly abundantly more than I could have asked or imagined. We also have four beautiful, well-mannered, and generous grandchildren.

I know God has answered our prayers for our children and will continue to, as well as now for our grandchildren, because we have based our prayers on God's Word, which is His will for us. We have obeyed God's Word and in faith prayed, believed, and spoken His will on earth as it is in heaven, and we have seen it come to pass. Of course we have had some bumps in the road, some hard spots to work through, but our life and our children's lives have been built on the foundation of His words—a very solid rock to be built upon. You, too, can build your life and the lives of your children and grandchildren as you pray God's Word and will for them regularly. Let it be written, and let it be done.

Take a Step

Get several Scriptures together to pray for your children according to the things they are facing in their lives right now. Pray and speak those over them regularly.

Lean In

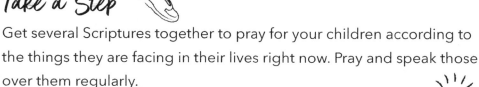

Father, help me to be consistent in praying for each of my children, knowing you have the perfect plan for them. Protect them in Jesus's name against any and all schemes of the enemy that would try to kill, steal, or destroy them in any way and in any form in their lives.

Digging Deeper

- *While They Are Sleeping: 12 Character Traits to Pray for Your Child* by Ann Arkins and Gary Harrell. There are many Scriptural references for each trait, "you and me" time activities for connecting with your child, and a "live it" section for each trait with innovative ways you can practically develop a trait together.
- *Prayers and Promises for My Little Boy* by Stormie Omartian
- *Prayers and Promises for My Little Girl* by Stormie Omartian
- *Warrior Prayers: Praying the Word for Boys in the Areas They Need It Most* by Brooke L. McGlothlin

"The closest I get to a spa day is when the steam from the dishwasher smacks me in the face!"

Notes

To Do, or Not to Do

> *Whatever you do, do it heartily,*
> *as to the Lord and not to men.*
> **COLOSSIANS 3:23 NKJV**

Is your to-do list a mile long? Do you ever cross off or complete every item on your list in a day? Sometimes it seems like there is no way to get everything that needs to be done in a single day finished. There are already so many expectations on us as parents, and yet we still add so much to our already overloaded plates. I have been there.

When my kids were little, I often had unrealistic expectations, with a daily to-do list that was almost impossible. I tend to be a goal setter, so a daily list was a natural thing for me. The only problem with the list was that it was way too long. The items I put down on the list should have been for a week, not a day!

Every night when the day was over, I found myself with a sense of frustration rather than a feeling of accomplishment. Soon, my list became more important than interacting or playing with the kids. As most parents know, we have a constant fight to maintain a balance between work, running our household, giving attention to our spouse and children, and still trying to find time for ourselves. I have good news—there is hope!

It's time to scale back our lofty expectations and make a to-do list that is actually feasible. Novel idea, right? Some of you reading this might not be in the habit of making daily lists or schedules, but I highly recommend it. For others, list making and goal setting are part of your DNA. No matter which group you are in, you can find the balance between people (our kids) and tasks (all the to-dos).

The secret to everything in life is balance, and as parents, we have to adapt to interruptions. What you might think is a fifteen-minute job or task can take an hour— or longer if you must stop to change a diaper, referee an argument, or fix a snack. The key is to not overplan your day! If you are a stay-at-home mom with little preschoolers, one or two outings a day is plenty. If you work outside the home, getting everyone dressed and out the door in time is a major accomplishment. For those moms working outside the home (as well as inside the home), you might try running errands during your lunch hour or on your way home so you don't have to do them once you get home from work. Another fix for working moms is to do one chore each evening to try to keep up with housework and to free up some of your time on the weekend.

Look for resources online about how to simplify life. You can find meal planners with grocery lists, grocery ordering apps, and thousands of other things. I have seen calendars that display each day of the month and list two or three small chores to accomplish that day. When you have a very busy life, it is so worthwhile to find a few tools that organize areas of your life for you. Utilize programs that already exist to bring order to your life.

If you have a little extra cushion in your budget, it might be worth hiring a cleaning service to come to your house once or twice a month. Another option is to hire someone who you know needs a little extra money to handle tasks you don't have time to do. Hiring someone can really alleviate a lot of the pressure and stress from your schedule and help knock a few things off your list. I learned this years ago and have since been able to employ some of the youth at our church to come on the weekends or after school and help with cleaning and organizing projects. This is a great help for projects you really need to do but don't have time to do, like organizing the pantry, cleaning and organizing the garage, going grocery shopping, or planting flowers. Also, get your kids involved. Are there things you are doing around your house your kids are completely capable of doing? It is healthy and helpful for kids to have chores.

Two of the most important things to remember to do, whether you are a stay-at-home mom or a working mom outside the home, is to plan ahead and map your time. Again, there are so many great, helpful resources online. You can look up articles on time-management tips and simple ways to organize your home as well as ways to help simplify your to-do list. There are also so many excellent tips on Pinterest, including lists of chores for kids at every age.

I remember my mom telling me many times to enjoy my children, to take time to play with them and give them my full attention because they grow and change so quickly. I am now a grandmother, and it seems like only ten minutes ago that my children were the age my grandkids are now. I did savor the moments, but time has no mercy and keeps a relentless, fast pace.

Now my house is clean and in order—two things I used to think were the most important items of the day. A season in your life is coming soon where there won't be any toys to put away or diapers to change. Your house and your time will be yours alone, but for now, pour into your children with your love and attention. You represent God's fatherly love to them.

I saw this post on Facebook and thought it was powerful: "Imagine our children saying, 'We know God because we saw God's love in our parents, and that equipped us to live a fearless life.'"

Take a Step

Take a few minutes to identify if there are reoccurring tasks on your list that just never seem to get finished. Are these tasks something you can outsource to an app, a service, or a person you can pay? Do you know friends or family members who could use a little extra money? Hire them to do some of your tasks that never seem to get done. Ordering your groceries through an app not only saves time but also saves money because you are not in store to make those impulse purchases. Look up a list of age-appropriate tasks for your kids to complete on a daily or weekly basis, and incentivize them with a small allowance or reward.

Lean In

Father, I am so thankful that you are my ever-present help in time of need. I need your help right now. Show me how to simplify my to-do list so it is manageable and fruitful. I don't want to be so caught up in the minutiae of life that I miss the chance to love the people around me. I also want to make sure I am seeking you first and finding rest and energy in you. I know that as I focus on you, you bring me the insight and wisdom I need to successfully run my household. Help me be the most effective, productive person possible while still leading my family with joy and peace. In Jesus's name, amen.

"Being home with kids all day is just the loneliest never-alone thing: like living in a cave filled with malfunctioning."

TEDDY RUXPINS

In Closing

Even though I have written and encouraged you to savor the moments because they go so fast, I realize that not every moment is enjoyable as a parent. It wasn't for me, and it often won't be for you. And that is okay. Parenting is such hard work, and it is a 24-7 job. I remember some days I wanted to run away because I was so tired of the routine and felt like I wasn't accomplishing much. I was blessed to have my mom and dad, as well as my mother and father-in-law, in town to help relieve us and keep the children overnight sometimes. My sister-in-law, Sally Ann, also traded off in keeping our children from time to time, which was wonderful. Hopefully, even if you don't have family in town, you have one friend who can keep your children, and then you keep theirs. We also used a few girls from our church to babysit for us for date nights. Steve Wiens gives us a little humor:

Let me be the one who says the following things out loud:

You are not a terrible parent if you can't figure out a way for your children to eat as healthy as your friend's children do. She's obviously used a bizarre and probably illegal form of hypnotism.

You are not a terrible parent if you yell at your kids sometimes. You have little dictators living in your house. If someone else talked to you like that, they would be put in prison. . . .

You are not a terrible parent if you would rather be at work [some days, or are already at work].

You are not a terrible parent if you just can't wait for them to go to bed [some days].

You are not a terrible parent.

You are an actual parent with limits. You cannot do it all. We all need to admit that one of the causalities specific to our information saturated culture is that we have sky-scraper standards for parenting.[1]

It is by God's grace in each of our lives that He gives us wisdom and stamina, when we depend on Him, to do this wonderful and selfless thing called parenting. There were so many days when my children were small that it felt like a thankless, endless job. I was accustomed to getting kudos at work, and the children were just too young to say, "Thanks, Mom," for that hundredth diaper change, or "Thanks for instilling in me the concept of sharing with my brother when I really didn't want to." We don't get instant gratification or a bonus as we repetitively, minute by minute pour into their lives the little lessons that build character in them and help them know how to make good choices.

In so many ways, we parent by faith, knowing what we are doing is having a lasting and life-changing influence on our children, but we're not instantly seeing how all of it works out for good. It's day after day, week after week, year after year of living to the best of our ability and

---

1   Steve Wiens, "To parents of small children: Let me be the one who says it out loud" (emphasis original), *Steve Wiens* (blog), March 12, 2013, https://stevewiens.com/2013/03/12/to-parents-of-small-children-let-me-be-the-one-who-says-it-out-loud/.

God's ability in us, a life that keeps Jesus in the center of it all, and His words of faith and life pouring out on our little ones.

> Yet all of the accomplishments that I once took credit for, I've now forsaken them and I regard it as nothing compared to the delight of experiencing Jesus Christ as my Lord!
> **PHILIPPIANS 3:7 TPT**

Digging Deeper

· Steve Wiens, "To parents of small children: Let me be the one who says it out loud" at Stevewiens.com.

A Prayer for Those Who Would Like to Know Jesus

Dear heavenly Father,

I come to you in the name of Jesus.

Your Word says, "The one who comes to Me I will by no means cast out" (John 6:37), so I know you won't cast me out. You take me in, and I thank you for it.

You said in your Word, "Whoever calls on the name of the Lord shall be saved" (Romans 10:13). I am calling on your name, so I know you have saved me now.

You also said, "If you confess with your mouth the Lord Jesus and believe in your heart that God has raised Him from the dead, you will be saved. For with the heart one believes unto righteousness, and with the mouth confession is made unto salvation" (Romans 9:9-10). I believe in my heart Jesus Christ is the Son of God. I believe that He was raised from the dead for my justification, and I confess Him now as my Lord.

Because your Word says, "With the heart one believes unto righteousness," and I do believe with my heart, I have now become the righteousness of God in Christ (2 Corinthians 5:21) and I am saved!

Thank you, Lord!

About the Author

PHOTOS BY MEGAN KAMAUOHA

Sheri Schaefer was born in Oklahoma and raised in Santa Fe, New Mexico, until her college years, when her parents moved to Albuquerque. She met her husband, Mike, while attending the University of New Mexico and later graduated with a husband and a master's degree. Today, Mike and Sheri have two adult children (who are married to amazing, loving spouses), and they adore their four grandchildren.

Sheri is passionate about teaching on parenting, marriage, and faith. She and Mike have pastored Church Alive! since 1995. When they are not pastoring they love to travel, ski, scuba dive, snorkel, hang out at the beach, and read. Taking mission trips into China and Thailand has enriched their lives and expanded their love for people.

Connect with Sheri for Speaking Engagements:

· Email: PastorSheri@ChurchAliveABQ.com
· Instagram: @SheriSchaef; Facebook.com/Sheri.Schaefer.9

About the Co-Author

PHOTO BY MORRELL PHOTOGRAPHY

Meg Schaefer was born in St. Louis and grew up in Oklahoma and Indiana. She attended college at Purdue University and Oklahoma State university. Meg settled in Tulsa and met her husband, Shaun Schaefer, at their church, Guts Church. They have two daughters, Drew Paige and Beau Elizabeth.

Meg is a freelance writer and editor, and has extensive experience in advertising and marketing. Shaun, Meg and their girls are very involved at their church and with school activities and sports. They love adventuring with both sides of their family and their incredible friends.

Made in the USA
Monee, IL
12 November 2024

69958232R00115